Devotional Commentary on PHILIPPIANS

F.B. Meyer Memorial Library

Devotional Commentary on Exodus

Choice Notes on Joshua to 2 Kings

Choice Notes on the Psalms

Devotional Commentary on Philippians

Devotional Commentary on PHILIPPIANS

by

F.B. Meyer

KREGEL PUBLICATIONS
Grand Rapids, Michigan 49501

First Kregel Publications edition 1979
Reprinted 1984

Library of Congress Cataloging in Publication Data

Meyer, Frederick Brotherton, 1847-1929.
Devotional Commentary on Philippians.

(F.B. Meyer Memorial Library)
Reprint of the ed. published by Religious Tract Society, London under title: The Epistle to the Philippians, in series: A devotional commentary.
1. Bible. N.T. Philippians — Commentaries. I. Bible. N.T. English. 1978. Devotional commentary on Philippians. 1978. II. Title. III. Series: A Devotional commentary.
BS2705.M4 1978. 227'.6'077 78-59146
ISBN 0-8254-3227-8

Printed in the United States of America

CONTENTS

PUBLISHER'S PREFACE

As a preacher, Dr. F. B. Meyer was welcomed by vast crowds in the largest churches. He was also a writer of outstanding ability and his expository books and the series of biographies of Bible characters have had a world-wide appeal.

The author shares his loyalty to the inspired Scriptures and ably applies valuable lessons to the needs of the Christian believer living under tension and facing the pressures of life. He possessed a rare combination of thorough scholarship and deep devotion to his Lord and Saviour. One feels the Lord's presence in his writings as though He is walking with you and teaching you.

Although this verse-by-verse commentary is both scholarly and exegetical, its devotional character makes it as much a blessing for the layman as for the Bible student. It provides practical instruction and spiritual direction for an effective Christ-centered life.

As the rays of the full moon reflect the light of the then-invisible sun and illumine one's nighttime journey, so the author here illumines the Christian's pathway for living and service with reflected truth from the ascended Son.

It is a privilege to make available this great

work to assist teachers, Bible students and pastors in their personal Bible study and message preparation.

THE PUBLISHERS

PREFACE

In this Devotional Commentary on the Epistle to the Philippians, I have not attempted anything of the merely critical or exegetical; but have endeavored honestly to ascertain the meaning of the Apostle, and to beat out his pure and unalloyed gold.

The most amazing thing which meets one perpetually in the prolonged and deep study of such a treatise as this, is that those early believers should have been able to appreciate and digest such compressed and profound teaching. When we bear in mind all the explanation, expansion, application, and enforcement which these apostolic paragraphs have received in the course of the centuries, and when, after we have done our best, we are still conscious that we have by no means plumbed the depths, or scaled the heights, or explored all the teasures, we are compelled to feel that the Divine Fire is burning here, and to take off the shoes from our feet in acknowledgment that in a pre-eminent manner, God is here. Every blue crevasse, every far horizon, every glimpse into a perfect human love, and every word of God has the same characteristic of *Infinity*.

To Dr. Moule, the Bishop of Durham, to my friend, Dr. Noble, of Chicago, and to Dr. Campbell

Morgan, for suggestions, which I have wrought into the seventh chapter (pp. 63-71), I desire to express my deep obligations.

It seems to me, if I may be allowed to say so, that this Book, more completely than any single one besides, contains the essence of the messages with which I have been entrusted.

That the Infinite Spirit who inspired may, by manifesting the Truth, unfold the deep things of God to all who peruse these pages is the sincere desire and prayer of the author.

F. B. MEYER.

1

THE VESTIBULE OF THE EPISTLE

Philippians 1:1,2

PAUL and Timotheus, the servants of Jesus Christ, to all the saints in Christ Jesus which are at Philippi, with the bishops and deacons:

Grace *be* unto you, and peace, from God our Father, and *from* the Lord Jesus Christ.

Phil. i. 1, 2

THIS is the tenderest of all the Epistles. There is no chiding or rebuke. It is suffused throughout with words of good cheer, of joy and peace, though it was written in bonds to which the Apostle makes frequent reference (i. 7, 13, 14, 16). There is no trace of despondency or gloom, and though sent to a Church which he had not seen for five or six years, there appeared no necessity for those strictures and reproofs with which the other Epistles are filled.

Date and Occasion of the Epistle

If, as is supposed, this Epistle was written at the beginning of Paul's imprisonment in Rome, we must assign to it *the date* A.D. 62. It is the beginning of the precious prison literature of the Church which is amongst our greatest treasures. It was a persecuted Apostle writing to a persecuted Church, but his soul was unfettered and unchoked by prison damp. Perhaps his hired house in its discomfort would compare favourably with the gaol at Bedford, which Bunyan describes as 'a den,' but the Apostle was

Phil. i. 1, 2

conscious, as Bunyan never was, of the daily clank of the chain which accompanied every movement.

The occasion of the writing of this Epistle is clearly indicated by the references which the Apostle makes. Philippi stood at the head of the Ægean Sea, about nine miles from the coast. Its earliest name was the Fountain City, afterwards it was enlarged by Philip, the king of Macedonia, and called after himself. It was the scene of the great battle between Brutus and Cassius on the one side, and Octavius and Antony on the other. In commemoration of the decisive victory of imperialism over republicanism, Augustus gave it the dignity and privilege of a Roman colony. It was, in fact, a miniature Rome, hence its consuls and lictors (Acts xvi. 20). The great Egnatian Way passed through it; and as a Roman colony situated on this great thoroughfare, it was flourishing and wealthy, though now it is a desolation, trodden only by the traveller and shepherd.

The Apostle had been brought there in answer to the vision of the man of Macedonia, but had met with a poor response. His first sermon was preached to a few devout Jews, especially women, who, unable to erect a synagogue, were wont to gather by the riverside on the Sabbath day. The story of the opening of Lydia's heart, and the subsequent formation of a Christian Church, which was favoured with two visits on the part of the Apostle, is too well-known to need detailed retelling.

Epaphroditus, whom the Philippians had sent with their greeting and pecuniary assistance, had fallen ill during his stay at Rome, and as the tidings of this misfortune caused great anxiety to his fellow-disciples, on his recovery the Apostle hastened his return and entrusted to his care messages of gratitude and affection; hurrying him back, that by his presence he might dissipate the anxiety which had cast a gloom over the entire Christian community. Phil. i. 1, 2

It is sufficient to say that this Epistle has received unmistakable testimony as to its authenticity and genuineness. It is referred to by Ignatius and Polycarp, quoted by Clement, Irenæus, and Tertullian, and bears in its texture abundant evidence of having issued from the heart and mind of the great Apostle to the Gentiles.

* * *

'Paul and Timothy, bond-servants of Christ Jesus'

Years before, when quite a youth, Timothy had been brought to Christ on Paul's first visit to Lystra. Having been well instructed by his mother, Eunice, and his grandmother, Lois, when Christ was presented as the fulfilment of the Old Testament by Paul, he received Him with all the ardour of young manhood. The Apostle ever after considered him as 'his own son in the faith.' During the seven following years he grew in knowledge and love, and on Paul's second visit he was judged capable of accompanying him, and sharing his hardships and labours on behalf of the Gospel.

The two names are associated in 2 Corinthians, Colossians, Philippians, and 1 and 2 Thessalonians, and we can never forget the touching last letter which the Apostle dictated to him from the Mamertine prison on the eve of martyrdom. It is worthy

Phil. i. 1, 2

of notice that the Apostle, who will presently refer to the saints at Philippi, classes himself with Timothy as the '*bond-slaves* of Christ Jesus.' There is no assumption, no priestly prerogative, no pretentiousness in this simple designation. Though the Apostle had much in which he might glory, when he reviewed the work of his crowded life, he had so great an estimate of his Master, Christ, that in His presence he took the lowliest place;—the bought chattel of Him who had purchased him, not with corruptible things, but with His precious Blood. Men would have little fault to find with the ministers of the Churches, if they breathed the same spirit of simplicity, humility, and abandonment to the will of the great Master.

* * *

Saints and Saintship

'*To all the saints in Christ Jesus which are at Philippi, with the bishops* (R.V. marg. overseers) *and deacons.*' The word 'saint' is frequently used by the Apostle, in the opening words of the Epistles. In that to the Romans, he describes believers as 'called to be saints.' So in 1 Cor. i. 2, see also Eph. i. 1; Col. i. 2. We are not to infer from this that they were perfect in character, but that they were set apart from the world, by the cross of Christ and the anointing of the Holy Spirit, for high and holy service in the world. Men use this term of the departed, and canonise their fellow-believers only after many years have elapsed since they passed to the service of the eternal world. But the Apostle did not hesitate to describe very imperfect men and women, who needed a large amount of tuition and admonition, as saints; thus imputing to them God's great ideal, as perhaps the likeliest means of inspiring them to deserve the title. Phil. i. 1, 2

Is not this a true way of dealing with men? Do not be content with rebuking them when they do wrong, but lay your hand upon their shoulder, and tell them that you are sure that they are capable of better things, that the angel lies hidden in the marble, that the possibility of saintship is deep down in the soul, in virtue of the regenerating grace of the Spirit, who is forming Christ within. Thus you will inspire hope, resolve, high purpose, and the resolute intention that the character and walk shall not fall beneath this great word with which God does not hesitate to designate all who are incorporated in a living union with His Son.

Would you be a saint indeed? Then live 'in Christ Jesus' as your King (*Christ*), and in Jesus in all the human relationship of daily life (*Jesus*). Let Him be your atmosphere and environment, your protection from the assaults of evil from without, and the sweet fragrance which will exhale through the inner sanctuary of your nature, in speech and act.

Bishops and Deacons

As to the 'bishops and deacons': 'There is now no question,' and this is endorsed by Bishop Ellicott, 'that in the Holy Scriptures, the two titles of "bishop" and "presbyter" are applied to the same person.' For this see Acts xx. 17, 28. Bishop Lightfoot affirms, 'It is a fact now generally recognised by theologians of all shades of opinion, that in the language of the New Testament the same officer in the Church is called indifferently "bishop," or

Phil. i. 1, 2

"elder," or "presbyter."' He goes on to say: 'The opinion hazarded by Theodoret, and adopted by many later writers, that the same officers in the Church who were first called apostles came afterwards to be designated bishops, is baseless." According to this dictum 'a New Testament bishop is a New Testament presbyter, and New Testament bishops and presbyters are simply ministers of Jesus Christ and pastors of churches.'

Dr Moule in his valuable book, *Philippian Studies*, says: 'It is important to remember that our word bishop cannot properly translate the Greek word as it is used in the New Testament, for it is not used there as the special title of a superintendent pastor set over other pastors.' For the office of deacon we have simply to refer to Acts vi. In the early Church there were evident ranks of gift, but not of grace. As believers gathered at the Lord's Table, or Love Feast, there was no distinction but that of humility and service. All were redeemed by the same Blood, stood on the same level; and each strove to be the lowliest and humblest of all.

* * *

The combined Salutation

'*Grace to you and peace from God our Father and the Lord Jesus Christ.*' Grace was the western, and Peace the eastern salutation. The Apostle combines them. He desired that his absent friends might know more and more of the free favour of God, of forgiveness and acceptance, and of the enjoyment of help and comfort. He would also have them know that peace which filled his own heart, amid trials of no ordinary description, and which was bequeathed by the Master,—'My peace I leave with you, My peace I give unto you.' Phil. i. 1, 2

Notice how closely he conjoins the Father and the Redeemer. He did not think that he was robbing God of His unity or supremacy when he included our Lord in the same sentence. Though all his early training had recognised the Oneness of the Divine Nature, he had no scruple in adding to God the Father the Lord Jesus Christ.

It is remarkable to notice also the number of times in which he mentions the Saviour's name. It occurs forty times in this Epistle, that is, on an average, in every two or three verses, but this is characteristic of the New Testament, and especially of the writings of this Apostle. He was a slave of Jesus Christ; he viewed all saints as living, with himself, in Christ; his life was full of Christ; Christ was his life; to die was to depart to be with Him; his rejoicing was in Christ Jesus; and steadfastness was only possible, as he and his converts stood fast 'in the Lord.' The Lord was always at hand to him, and because all believers were in Christ, they could count on God to supply all their need.

Let us rejoice to know that 'grace and peace' are not exhausted, but that they flow down to us still in this remote century, and amid the altered circumstances of modern life. Christ was, and is, and is to come. In Him the Church still exists, through Him she is still supplied with grace upon grace, and unto Him she will be gathered without spot, or wrinkle, or any such thing.

2

PRAYER AND INTERCESSION

Philippians 1:3,4

I THANK my God upon every remembrance of you,
Always in every prayer of mine for you all making request with joy.

Phil. i. 3, 4
The Prayers of St Paul

THE Epistles of St Paul are full of allusions to his prayers. We might almost call them his prayer-book. Let us verify that assertion by turning to the Epistles as they come on the pages of the Bible.

Rom. i. 9: 'God is my witness, whom I serve in my spirit in the Gospel of His Son, how unceasingly I make mention of you, always in my prayers making request,' etc.

1 Cor. i. 4: 'I thank my God always concerning you, for the grace of God which was given you in Christ.'

Eph. i. 16: 'I cease not to give thanks for you, making mention of you in my prayers.'

Eph. iii. 14: 'For this cause I bow my knees unto the Father.'

Col. i. 3: 'We give thanks to God, the Father of our Lord Jesus Christ, praying always for you.'

Col. ii. 1: 'I would have you know how greatly I strive for you, and for them at Laodicea, and for as many as have not seen my face in the flesh.'

Prayer and Intercession

1 Thess. i. 2: 'We give thanks to God always for you all, making mention of you in our prayers.' Phil. i. 3, 4

2 Thess. i. 11: 'To which end we also pray always for you.'

2 Tim. i. 3: 'I thank God, . . . how unceasing is my remembrance of thee.'

Philemon 4: 'I thank my God always, making mention of thee in my prayers.'

These texts are sufficient to substantiate the assertion that the Epistles of St Paul abound in allusions to his prayers on behalf of his converts; and just as our Lord Jesus Christ ever lives to intercede, so the true pastor, Sunday School teacher, or Christian friend, should day and night, without ceasing, remember the saved and unsaved of his charge in prayer.

Prayer: with tears and with joy

But there was a special liberty in the Apostle's prayer, for in verse 4 he says: 'Always in every supplication of mine, making my supplication *with joy.*' Those of us who know what it is to pray, are familiar with the alternations that come over the soul when it waits before God. There are some tracts and passages in our daily prayer-life which we tread with difficulty and tears. For those who seem so obdurate; for those who appear to have turned their backs determinedly upon God; for certain Churches that appear hopelessly desolate and barren, we plead with strong crying and tears. We tread these acres of our prayer-life, with weeping, sowing seed destined to bear an abundance of harvest fruit.

There are other parts of our daily prayer-life that are illumined with joy. When we come to pray for

Phil. i. 3, 4

a beloved child, for some kindred spirit, for some blessed work of God which enjoys the perpetual dew of His favour, then it is easy to pray, and we make our supplication and request with joy. We know exactly what St Paul meant, when he said that there was a liberty, a freedom, a gladness in prayer which suffused his heart as he prayed for the Philippians.

* * *

Our Private Prayers

Nothing would be better for most of us than a great revival in our habits of private prayer. We cannot do as Luther, who was accustomed to say, 'I have so much work to do to-day that I cannot get through it with less than three hours of prayer'; or as Bishop Andrewes, who regularly set apart five hours each day for private devotion; or as Law, the author of the *Serious Call,* who was accustomed, as the clock rang out each third hour, to turn to prolonged prayer, allocating to each occasion some special subject. Our habits of life, and perhaps our methods of thought, forbid our adopting anything quite so absorbing and prolonged; but that we should pray more, that we should labour in prayer as Epaphras did, that we should cultivate the art of prayer, is clear.

Cultivate the Habit

Habits of prayer need careful cultivation. The instinct and impulse are with us by the grace of the Holy Spirit, but we need to cultivate the gracious inward movements until they become solidified into an unbending practice.

As far as possible, we should set apart one period in each day for prayer, and there can be no question that the *morning hour* is best. When the body is fresh from sleep, and before the rush of daily thought, care, and activity invades the mind, ere we hold intercourse with our nearest and dearest, *then* the bells ring for matins, and it is wise to heed their call. **Phil. i. 3, 4**

'Give Him thy first thoughts
So shalt thou keep
Him company all day
And in Him sleep.'

Use an Oratory

It is good, also to have *an oratory.* There should be, as far as possible, one room and one spot in the room, or one garden path, or a walk over the moor or beside the sea, where our seasons of private devotion are spent, and our prayers are wont to be made. The posture is a secondary matter. Many a heaven-moving prayer has been uttered whilst the feet have been plodding along the road, or the hands plying their toils, or when weakness has chained the body to the couch. Whilst Paul was floating for a night and a day in the deep, his soul was as much wrapt in the spirit of prayer as when he was in a trance in the temple.

A rich man, visited by his pastor, was in sore distress because when praying during the night he had not removed his nightcap. His scruples were, however, allayed by the wise and skilful reply, 'Some people pray, as Christians mostly do, with their shoes on and their heads uncovered; others, like the Jews and Mohammedans, pray with their heads covered and their shoes off. Now, I daresay, my friend, when you prayed, you had not your shoes on?' 'No, sir, I hadn't,' was the eager answer, and the troubled soul

Phil. i. 3, 4

was comforted. But it would have been better far if it had never been troubled. It is of real service to have the fixed closet, and the habitual attitude there; but it is a great mistake to magnify any of these accidents and circumstances as though they were essential.

Seek a Spirit of Prayer

The main point for each of us is to have a spirit of prayer, so that the exercise be not irksome and tedious, but that the spirit may spring to it with delight. We must not, however, wait for the high tide to rise before we launch forth on the voyage. If there is not deep water, we must make what use we can of the shallows. If we cannot step off to the big ship, we must make for it in the little boat which draws only a foot or two of water. If the gale is not blowing to fill our flagging sails, we must make what use we can of the light breezes that dimple the calm and lethargic ocean. Good is it when the soul leaps towards the prayer-hour, as a child to mother, or wife to husband; but failing this eager desire, let us pray because we ought, and because the supreme Lover of Souls will be disappointed if we do not appear at the trysting-place to keep our appointment.

The ways by which the sluggish soul can be incited to pray are various, and hints may be jotted down here which will be useful.

When the hour for prayer arrives, allow time for staying on the threshold of the temple, to remember how great God is, how greatly He is to be praised, how great your needs are. Remember the distance between you and Him, and be sure that it is filled with love. Recall the promises that bid you to approach. Consider all the holy souls that have entered and are entering those same portals; and do not forget the many occasions in which the lowering skies have cleared, the dark clouds have parted, and weakness has become power during one brief spell of prayer. Phil. i. 3, 4

A still greater need

We specially need the aid of the Holy Spirit, who helps our infirmities in prayer. He kindled the spark of devotion at the first, and knows well how to fan it into a flame. It is good to confide in Him, to confess that you would but cannot pray, that your desires are languid and your love cool, that the lips which should be touched with fire are frost-bitten, that the wings which ought to have borne you to Heaven are clipped. He understands and loves to be appealed to, and will assuredly quicken the flagging soul until it shall mount up as on eagle wings, running without wearying, and walking without faintness. One look to the Spirit of Prayer will find Him in the heart. As our Teacher He begins to repeat the words of petition, which we lisp after Him. As our Comforter and Paraclete He stands beside us, showing us where to aim our petitions, and steadying our trembling hands. As the Spirit of Life, he makes us free from the law of sin and death.

> 'Felt art Thou, and relieving tears
>   Fall, nourishing our young resolves;
> Felt art Thou, and our icy fears
>   The sunny smile of love dissolves.'

Helps to Prayer

It is advisable to use the Bible specially, and afterwards some spirit-stirring book, be it memoir

Phil. i. 3, 4

or spiritual treatise, to stir up the black hot coals and compel them to break into a heaven-ascending flame. The story of George Muller, of James Gilmour, or of David Brainerd, the writings of Samuel Rutherford, Andrew Murray and Frances Ridley Havergal, the poetry of Horatius Bonar and John Keble, are of perennial use in this direction.

Sometimes it will be the confession of recent backsliding and inconsistency, which have drawn a veil over the face of Christ; sometimes the overflowing of thanksgiving, as you count over your blessings, one by one; sometimes the urgency of need to intercede for some beloved friend or friends; but always, if you look for it, you may discover some wave of blessed helpfulness, which, flowing up on the shore of your life, will, as it recedes, afford you an opportunity of passing out with it from the high and dry stones to the bosom of the heaving ocean.

A Condition of Successful Prayer

One condition of successful prayer must never be forgotten. We must *believe* that God is, and that He is the rewarder of them that diligently seek Him. The Father is the object of our prayer, through the mediation of our Lord Jesus, and by the aid of the Holy Spirit; but however we conceive of it, whether the Father, or the Son, or the Holy Spirit, is the prominent object before our thought, we must believe that there is an eye that witnesses our poor endeavours, an ear that listens, a mind that can be impressed and affected by our requests. But further, we need a living faith which reckons on the faithfulness of God, and believes that it has already received its petitions, when they are founded on specific promises and evidently prompted by the Holy Spirit. **Phil. i. 3, 4** When we pray, it is not enough merely to speak a long list of requests into the ear of God, it becomes us to wait after each one, and to receive by an appropriating act of the soul. It is as though we saw God take from the shelves of His storehouse the boon on which we had set our heart, label it with our name, and put it aside until the precise moment arrived in which He could bestow it on us without hurt. But whether it is in our hands or not is of small matter, because 'we *know* that we have the petitions that we desired of Him.' Well may George Herbert sing:—

> 'Oh, what an easy, quick access,
> My blessed Lord, art Thou ! how suddenly
> May our requests Thine ear invade !
> To show that state dislikes not easiness.
> If I but lift mine eyes, my suit is made :
> Thou canst no more not hear, than Thou canst die.
>
> 'Since then these three wait on Thy throne,
> Ease, power, and love ; I value prayer so,
> That, were I to leave all but one,
> Wealth, fame, endowments, virtues, all should go :
> I and dear prayer would together dwell,
> And quickly gain, for each inch lost, an ell.'

3

THE GROUNDS AND PURPOSES OF THE PRAYER

Philippians 1:5-11

FOR your fellowship in the gospel from the first day until now;

Being confident of this very thing, that He which hath begun a good work in you will perform *it* until the day of Jesus Christ:

Even as it is meet for me to think this of you all, because I have you in my heart; inasmuch as both in my bonds, and in the defence and confirmation of the gospel, ye all are partakers of my grace.

For God is my record, how greatly I long after you all in the bowels of Jesus Christ.

And this I pray, that your love may abound yet more and more in knowledge and *in* all judgment;

That ye may approve things that are excellent; that ye may be sincere and without offence till the day of Christ;

Being filled with the fruits of righteousness, which are by Jesus Christ, unto the glory and praise of God.

Phil. i. 5-11

A Consciousness of Kinship

THE ground of his intercession was threefold. First, it arose from *his consciousness of their kinship.* We find this in verse 5: 'I make supplication with joy for your fellowship.' The Greek word there is *going shares—having in common*:—'I make supplication with joy because of your fellowship in furthering the Gospel.' (See also verse 7.)

It was the consciousness that those for whom he prayed were so closely akin to him in their determination and aims, that quickened the wheels of his supplication. Had they not shown this fellowship by sending repeatedly to his necessity, as we learn from the close of this Epistle? The Philippian Church, though very poor, had sent again and again generous gifts to supply the Apostle's wants, and this proved that they and he were animated with the same determination. Phil. i. 5-11

But more than this, there was the wireless telegraphy which bore out to the storm-tossed ship of his life the prayer and sympathy of his converts. For us also there are kindred spirits in different parts of the world, who are able by their prayer to send vibrations of holy energy into our souls, and when we pray for such we are able to make supplication with joy.

Living with God

Secondly, *the Apostle recognised that he was in the line of God's purpose.* This always makes it easy to pray. 'Being confident of this very thing, that He which began a good work in you will perfect it until the day of Jesus Christ.' He mentions two days in these verses—'From the first day,' and 'the day of Jesus Christ,'—and he says that between those two days, God, who began the work on the first day, and who will perfect it on the last day, is maintaining and building it up step by step.

That first day of our Christian life was due to the interposition of the grace of God. 'In the beginning God created.' The longer we live, the more sure we are that the beginning of the good work within must be attributed to God. No pastor, no mother, no teacher began it, but in the depth of our heart, by His Holy Spirit, God laid the first foundation stone of the new life, and amid all our sins, failures, and backslidings, He has been building up the

Phil. i. 5-11

work He commenced, and He cannot leave it. At Baalbec we find the remains of unfinished temples which man has abandoned half complete; but nowhere in the universe do we find unfinished worlds, half-made suns left incomplete, though many in the making. We go into the artist's studio and find there unfinished pictures covering large canvas, and suggesting great designs, but which have been left, either because the genius was not competent to complete the work, or because paralysis laid the hand low in death; but as we go into God's great workshop we find nothing that bears the mark of haste or insufficiency of power to finish, and we are sure that the work which His grace has begun, the arm of His strength will complete. It is easy to pray for a soul when you know that God also is at work perfecting it.

Impelled by Affection

Thirdly, *His tender affection towards them* (vv. 7,8). He says: 'I have you in my heart . . . and God is my witness, how I long after you all in the tender mercies of Christ Jesus.' The Apostle had got so near the very heart of his Lord that he could hear its throb, detect its beat, nay, it seemed as though the tender mercies of Jesus to these Philippians were throbbing in his own heart.

Let us live like this. You have children in your schools that greatly trouble you, boys and girls whose restless and obstinate natures seem to resist every overture; men and women meet you daily in your home-life, whom you cannot love with the love of natural affection; but, let every one of us get back to the heart of Jesus Christ until it pours its contents into ours, until we begin to yearn over the lost with the compassions of Jesus. Before you pass round that unkind story, before you say you will never speak to that man again, before you treat another with distance and coldness, get back to the heart of Jesus Christ, until His tender compassions shall fill yours. Then you can make supplication with joy. **Phil. i. 5-11**

* * *

Subject Matter of the Prayer

He says in verse 9: 'This I pray, that your love may abound yet more and more.' The Greek word is—That your love shall pour over—as the bucket which stands under a streamlet issuing from a fissure in the rocks pours over on all sides; I pray, he says, that your love may pour over towards each other, and specially towards God. Oh, that we might know this and be perfected in love, that there might be room for nothing more, that this might affect our whole being; for, depend upon it, when the love of God really fills the heart, the accent of the voice, the movements of our body, the look on the face, the demeanour, everything is affected. Too often we show the worried expression, the querulous tone, the over-strained nervous system, but through all this the love ought to pour, carrying away the discontented gloomy look, so that when we return to our dear ones at the close of the day, the entire household may feel that because we have come, sunlight and the love of God are flooding the house, which during the day had missed the music of our presence. Let 'your love abound yet more and more.'

'In all knowledge.' When this love enters a man's heart he *knows*. 'Everyone that loveth is

Phil. i. 5-11

born of God, and knoweth God.' Words infinitely deep, but corroborated here, because our Apostle prays that their love may abound more and more in all knowledge and discernment. When the fishers had tossed all night and taken nothing, and the grey dawn was breaking on the beach, it was the eye of him that loved which discerned the figure of the Master standing beside the fire of coals, and *John* said to Peter, 'It is the Lord.' If your love abounds more and more, you will not only know, but you will discern, you will be able to detect the traces of the footsteps of your Lord where other men fail to detect them, and hear His voice amid the jangling mart and the hubbub of the city.

* * *

Results: Discrimination

The effect of that love will be threefold. (1) *Discrimination.* 'That you may discriminate between things that differ' (v. 10, marg. R.V.). Such, without doubt, is the true rendering of the Greek, and we are reminded of Isaiah's words, which predict that the Spirit of the Lord shall rest upon the Messiah, and make Him 'of quick understanding.' The margin gives it *quick of scent.* When one has been on the ocean for a week, breathing the pure ozone, it is marvellous how quick one is to detect poisonous smells. This is well, and if we were quicker of scent, and detected the noisome effluvia which indicate corruption and disease, we should more certainly be saved from taking the poison into our systems. A man who has lost the sense of smell may go into the midst of disease without knowing it, but the man who is quick of scent is warned of danger. And the soul that loves deeply is marvellously quick to detect anything which may hurt or offend the loved one. It is so with the nature that loves God. It discerns, it discriminates, and amid the darkness or the grey dawn of our life, when things are so mixed, that they appear like one another, though really different, the love that loves God perfectly, discerns, and distinguishes between things that differ. A man's growth in grace is indicated by the delicacy of the discrimination that rules in his life. As he gets nearer God he detects in himself habits, and practices, ways of behaviour, and of business, which he once permitted without seeing evil in them, but now puts aside as unfit, to follow only the good. This is the first effect of perfected love. **Phil. i. 5-11**

(2) *Sincerity.* 'That you may be sincere and without offence' (v. 10). Just as the X-rays passing through the limb will show at once the fracture, or the result of some accident, so the X-rays of God's truth are always searching the heart, and when a man is living in perfect love, he also lives in perfect truth, for love and truth are one; and the man who lives in love does not mind meeting the searching rays of God's truth, which show that he is no hypocrite. **Results: Sincerity**

(3) *Fruitfulness.* It makes us 'full of the fruits of righteousness which are through Jesus Christ' (v. 11). An orchard is fair to see in the spring when there is promise of the blossom, but it is fairest in autumn, when every tree is laden to the ground with fruit. Let us seek this. The pruning is ever going on; the sunshine, and rain; but the whole **Results: Fruitfulness**

Phil. i. 5-11

discipline is making you full of luscious fruit, that thirsty souls may come to partake of the ripe fruit of your life, and turn from you to glorify and praise God. Be sure that love unites the believer very closely with the true Vine, and to be in living unison with Christ involves that we shall bear much fruit.

But all this is only 'through Jesus Christ.' Do not concern yourself so much with the fruit end of the bough, but with the end of fibrous wood which is connected with the vine. See to it that you live always in union with Jesus Christ, for without Him, severed from Him, you can do nothing. Abide in Him, and let Him abide in you. Let the one agony of your life be to keep near to Jesus. See to it that every morning in your prayer you touch Him, that you meditate on the Bible, that all day the union is kept unbroken, so that the living Christ may pour through you the sap of His own vitality, and fill you with the fruits of righteousness.

Is this your life? It may be from to-day. If you have never become united to Jesus Christ, the Divine man, you may become so by one look of faith. Then go forth to bear the fruit of a holy life to the glory of God, so that your life may praise Him in concert with the seraphs around His Throne.

'Thy love, Thy joy, Thy peace
Continuously impart
Unto my heart,
Fresh springs that never cease,
But still increase.'

4

THE FURTHERANCE OF THE GOSPEL

Philippians 1:12-18

BUT I would ye should understand, brethren, that the things *which happened* unto me have fallen out rather unto the furtherance of the gospel;

So that my bonds in Christ are manifest in all the palace, and in all other *places*;

And many of the brethren in the Lord, waxing confident by my bonds, are much more bold to speak the word without fear.

Some indeed preach Christ even of envy and strife; and some also of good will:

The one preach Christ of contention, not sincerely, supposing to add affliction to my bonds:

But the other of love, knowing that I am set for the defence of the gospel.

What then? notwithstanding, every way, whether in pretence, or in truth, Christ is preached; and I therein do rejoice, yea, and will rejoice.

Phil. i. 12-18

Man's Purpose and God's Power

IN Psalm lxxvi., breathing courage and confidence, which exalts the mighty Sovereign of all and magnifies His mighty power, the Psalmist tells us that the wrath of man shall be made to praise God. The wicked may plot against God, seeking to injure His servants and obstruct the progress of His truth, and within certain limits they may appear to succeed; but when they expect to reap the harvest of their evil machinations, they suddenly find themselves put to the worse, and God takes all that they had meant for the suppression of the Gospel, to promote its progress and triumph. There are few

Phil. i. 12-18

instances establishing this fact more striking than the story of the Apostle, for the misfortunes which befell his human life, and the difficulties over which he was compelled to make progress, were used by God to promote the highest interests of that very Gospel which was so dear to his heart, and for which he suffered so much.

St Paul's yearning for Rome

How eagerly he set his heart upon reaching Rome! In the Epistle to the Roman Christians, he tells them that he hopes presently that he may see Rome, not only that he may comfort them and be comforted by them, but because Rome was the metropolis of the world. From the golden mile-stone that stood in the Forum the mighty roads emanated to the far East and West. What Jerusalem was during the one week of the Passover, Rome was always. The statesmen who filled her Senate would be commissioned to all parts of the known world as consuls and prætors; the soldiers who gathered in her barracks might be dispatched to the far Euphrates on the one hand, or the white cliffs of Britain on the other. To reach Rome seemed like standing in some telephonic centre, from which a whisper would reverberate to the ends of the world.

The Apostle Paul was a great strategist. He knew the value of cities; they were the head of waters, into which if seed were dropped the current would carry it everywhere. Therefore, as he had spoken in Jerusalem, the heart of Palestine; at Antioch, the heart of Syria; at Ephesus, the heart of Asia Minor; and at Athens, the heart of Greece, he was desirous of preaching at Rome also, the heart of the empire of the world. No doubt he expected to get there as to other places, paying his own passage, going freely, and being welcomed by the little Churches of the saints, which were beginning to shed their light amid the surrounding gloom. But it was not thus that Paul accomplished his life-purpose. He came to Rome a prisoner, his passage paid as a convict by the Roman Government; and the hatred of his enemies was the breath of the Almighty that wafted him to his chosen destination.

Phil. i 12-18

Thus, constantly, God allows men to rage madly against His Gospel up to a certain point, which may cause annoyance, inconvenience, and pain, but there is always a 'thus far and no further,' and the Gospel proceeds upon the very lines which God from all eternity had determined.

This wonderful truth, which is capable of almost endless application, meets with three very remarkable illustrations in this paragraph.

* * *

Paul's Imprisonment in its Effect upon the Soldiers

'My bonds became manifest in Christ throughout the whole prætorian guard, and to all the rest' (v. 13). It would be better translated—*to the whole circle of the imperial life-guards.* We are all familiar with the fact that the Apostle was chained to a Roman soldier during the entire term of his two year's imprisonment, the soldier being changed every six hours. What an exquisite torture this must have been to a sensitive nature like his! Bad enough never to be alone, but still worse to have to spend the long hours always in company with a man chosen from the Roman guard.

Phil. i. 12-18

In the Epistles of Ignatius, the good bishop of Antioch, who was entrusted to such guards to bring him from his see at Antioch to be thrown to the wild beasts, describes himself as fighting day and night with ten leopards, who, the more kindness was shown them, waxed worse and worse. Though we may well imagine that some of the soldiers chained to the Apostle may have been quiet and wistful men, eager to know the truth, yet, quite as likely, others would fill the room with ribald songs and jokes, and turn into blasphemous ridicule the words they heard the Apostle speak to those who came to visit him.

At times the hired room would be thronged with people, to whom the Apostle spoke words of life; and after they withdrew the sentry would sit beside him, filled with many questionings as to the meaning of the words which this strange prisoner spoke. At other times, when all had gone, and especially at night, when the moonlight shone on the distant slopes of Soracte, soldier and Apostle would be left to talk, and in those dark, lonely hours the Apostle would tell soldier after soldier the story of his own proud career in early life, of his opposition to Christ, and his ultimate conversion, and would make it clear that he was there as a prisoner, not for any crime, not because he had raised rebellion or revolt, but because he believed that He whom the Roman soldiers had crucified, under Pilate, was the Son of God and the Saviour of men. As these tidings spread, and the soldiers talked them over with one another, the whole guard would become influenced in sympathy with the meek and gentle Apostle, who always showed himself so kindly to the men as they shared, however involuntarily, his imprisonment. **Phil. i. 12-18**

The witness of the Consistent Life

How absolutely consistent the Apostle must have been! If there had been the least divergence, day or night, from the high standard which he upheld, his soldier-companion would have caught at it, and passed it on to others. The fact that so many became earnest Christians, and that the Word of Jesus was known far and wide throughout the prætorian guard, indicates how absolutely consistent the Apostle's life was. Do you not see how this applies to your own life? You may be bound to unsympathetic companions, as the Apostle to his soldier, as Ignatius to his ten leopards, or as Nicholas Ridley, afterwards Bishop and martyr, to the bigoted Roman Catholic Mayor of Oxford; but by your meek consistency and purity of life you may win these for God, and what might therefore have appeared an obstacle to your growth in grace, and to the progress of the Gospel, may turn out just the opposite. See to it that you so live and speak that it may be so.

* * *

The Imprisonment: its Effect upon the Brethren

'Most of the brethren in the Lord, being confident through my bonds, are more abundantly bold to speak the word of God without fear' (v. 14). That is, courage was supplied them by the striking example of this noble man. Many who realised that, notwithstanding his chains and bonds, he was as enthusiastic in spreading the Gospel as he had

Phil. i. 12-18 been when his life was at his own disposal, and that, in spite of every difficulty and obstacle, he was still doing so much for the Gospel he loved, were rebuked for their lack of zeal and said: 'If the Apostle is so strong and brave and energetic, when there is every reason for him to slacken and mitigate his energy, how much more reason there is for us, who have unrestrained liberty of action, to be unceasing in our endeavours for that Gospel for which he suffers.'

The man who works for Christ when everything is against him stirs those up who have no such difficulties; just as he who makes confession for truth and righteousness, when there are many reasons for him to hush his voice, incites others to break forth in confession of Jesus Christ. They who dare to speak for God, even to death, are the means of stirring others to heroic defence of the Gospel. Think, for instance, of one of the greatest men that ever lived in England—a man whose name is almost forgotten now, but who is immortally associated with the cadence and splendid diction of the Bible—William Tyndale. It was his avowed purpose that every plough-boy in England should be able to know as much of the Bible as the priests. To accomplish this he appealed to the Bishop of London, but received no sympathy, and sorrowfully discovered that England could not hold the translator of the Bible. He was compelled to flee from England to Hamburg, from Hamburg to Cologne, from Cologne to Worms, and finally to Antwerp, where he was executed as a martyr; but not before he had put his imprimatur upon the magnificent English of the

Bible, and had invested the Scriptures with priceless interest for the minds and hearts of those who had watched his noble life, his beneficent career, and his bloody death, so that out of his ashes there sprang a hundred, nay, a thousand men, to scatter the Bible for which he died.

Phil. i. 12-18

A Call to you

This may also be the case with you who are called to suffer for the Gospel. It may seem as if your voice were being hushed in blood and tears; but others are being made bold. Many a young man in that worldly society or godless counting-house is saying 'If *he* dares to stand for God, I too will be a hero'; so that the very effect of your example is to stimulate weaker ones to become confessors and martyrs for Jesus Christ. Has not this been the result of the wholesale martyrdoms of Chinese missionaries and converts?

* * *

The Imprisonment: its Effect upon the Opponents of Evangelical Truth

'Some indeed preach Christ even of envy and strife, and some also of goodwill.' 'What then? Only that in every way, whether in pretence or in truth, Christ is proclaimed; and therein I rejoice, yea, and will rejoice' (v. 15, 18). There were two parties in Rome. The one loved Paul enthusiastically, and accepted his teaching; the other, though professedly Christian, held by the Temple, the Pharisees, and the old restrictions of Judaism. They avowed Christ, but often looked backward to the Old Covenant, and tried to weave the two together. Paul's coming aroused these to more earnestness in promoting their own views of Christianity, but he said: 'It does not matter, if Christ is preached;

Phil. i. 12-18

they do not love me, they do not come to me for help, they are doing all they can to make my life difficult; but nevertheless, if my Lord Jesus Christ is being preached, I am more than thankful.' Perhaps that explains why God has permitted the various denominations to divide England between them. Perhaps it is better that it should be so, because one stirs up the other. It may be that the efforts of the Nonconformists stir to more activity the members of the Church of England, and *vice versa.* In any case the various doctrines of Christianity are more likely to be strongly enforced and maintained, when they underlie the very existence of a body of Christians, than if they were held in common by all.

All through the history of the world God has taken what seemed to be a hindrance and obstacle, and, if only His servants were patient and true to Him, has converted it into a pulpit from which they could better promulgate the truth. Remember how Nebuchadnezzar harried the Jews. It seemed as if the holy city was never again to wield an influence for good over the world; but the chosen people were scattered with their Scriptures throughout the world, and the word of God was magnified much more than it could have been by their concentration in their own city. The devil stirred up the Jews to murder Christ, but the grain of wheat which fell into the ground to die, no more abode alone, but has covered the world with the harvests of rich grain. The Emperors persecuted the early Church, but only drove the disciples everywhere preaching the Word. King Charles chased the Puritans out of England, but they landed on Plymouth Rock, and founded the great Christian commonwealth across the Atlantic. Out of the awful Civil War the conditions arose that made it possible for Abraham Lincoln to free the slave, and again the wrath of man turned out to further the Gospel of Jesus Christ.

Phil. i. 12-18

'Careless seems the great Avenger,
History's pages but record
One death-grapple, in the darkness,
'Twixt old systems and the Word.
Truth for ever on the scaffold,
Wrong for ever on the throne;
Yet that scaffold sways the future,
And, behind the dim unknown,
Standeth God within the shadow,
Keeping watch upon His own.'

So it may be with us

So it will be in our life. Let us begin to rejoice at difficulties, to rejoice when Satan rages. The power which is used against us, God will convert for our good; only let us always cherish the eager expectation and hope that Christ may be magnified in our body, whether by life or by death, whether by joy or by shame, whether by good fortune or by misfortune, whether by success or by failure. Christ, Christ, Christ, the Blessed Christ—not the Bible alone, not the creed alone, not doctrine alone, but Christ, Christ, Christ, always Christ manifested in our body, whether it be by life or by death.

Is Christ dear to you? Do you live for Him? Is the one passion and aim and purpose of your nature to glorify Him? Can you say: To me to

Phil. i. 12-18

live is Christ, and to die is gain? Oh, let us from to-day begin to live for this!

And if you are discouraged and disheartened, be of good cheer. When you are devoted to Christ, your very bonds will become electric chains through which the pulsations of energy shall go to others, and your very troubles will be pulpits from which you shall preach the unsearchable riches of Christ.

Storms cannot shipwreck the Gospel; they waft it forward. Its foes contrive ingenious devices to obstruct it, but they awake to discover that all they had done to hinder is used to help. The lines of rail and the rolling stock which the enemy elaborated for incursions of hostile intent, are found to be simply invaluable to bear forward the precious message of the Gospel they would overthrow. It will be found, doubtless, at the end of all things, that the beneficent purposes of God have not been hindered one whit, but promoted and fostered, by all that has been done to frustrate them. This is the mystery of God's providence—that, so far from being set aside by evil, evil helps by furnishing the material on which the fire of the Gospel feeds, and flames to the furthest limits of God's universe.

5

GOOD OUT OF EVIL

Philippians 1:19,20

For I know that this shall turn to my salvation through your prayer, and the supply of the Spirit of Jesus Christ.

According to my earnest expectation and *my* hope, that in nothing I shall be ashamed, but *that* with all boldness, as always, *so* now also Christ shall be magnified in my body, whether *it be* by life, or by death.

Phil. i. 19, 20

The Two Parties

As we have seen, there were two parties in Rome. The one was devoted to the Apostle, and were doing their best to help him in the preaching of the Gospel of our Lord. These disciples were imbued with the spirit of their master, and were carried along in the current of his own devotion. 'In his bonds, and in the defence and confirmation of the Gospel, they were all partakers with him of grace.' The work they did was of good-will and of love, because they knew that he was set for the defence of the Gospel.

The other party refused to accept the Gospel in its simplicity. They belonged to the Judaising party, and held that it was necessary for a man to pass through the ceremonies of the old covenant, in order to participate in the benefits of the new. Throughout his life the Apostle was constantly troubled by the presence of these men, and his stay in Rome seems to have stirred them up to still greater activity. They preached Christ of envy and strife, not sincerely,

Phil. i. 19, 20

but of faction, thinking to raise up affliction in his bonds.

But out of this aggravation of his anxieties he managed to extract a new-found joy, to quote his own inimitable words, 'What then? only that in every way, whether in pretence or in truth, Christ is proclaimed; and therein I rejoice, yea, and will rejoice.' When the heart is absolutely right with God, when God is the one great fact which underlies all facts, it is able to elicit joy for every circumstance in life, as musicians music from the roar of the torrent, and the rush of the storm.

It is a serious question which each should ask, Is God the underlying fact in my life? Do I detect His presence in every storm, shower, and sunbeam, in the dark night as well as in the day, in my losses and sorrows as well as in my halcyon hours of summer joy? To such an one every wind wafts argosies across the sea laden with blessing, dreaded evils pass him by without molestation, the very Judases of life bring cups which have been mixed by the Father's hand. When God is real to us, and we receive all things either by His permission or appointment, we can find occasions for joy where other men see unmitigated grief, chinks of blue in the dark sky, and songs in the night.

* * *

Why Paul Rejoiced For Christ was Proclaimed

Paul was glad, first because Christ was proclaimed. So long as that name was being passed from lip to lip, and enquiry was excited into all that it stood for, and men were beginning to feel after Him, if haply they might find Him as the Saviour from their sins, and the solution of life's mysteries, he was satisfied. Better half a loaf than no bread, and better the preaching of Christ from wrong motives than not at all. Better Christ pilloried than not lifted up before the thought of the time. A good man may be glad when the world's press deals with Christian truth, even though it be travestied and misrepresented, it is better thus than that men should lose interest in Christianity. Nothing is more fatal than apathy and neglect.

Phil. i. 19, 20

For all would turn out well

Paul rejoiced because he saw that everything would turn out right for him. 'I know that this shall turn to my salvation.' There has been a good deal of controversy as to what he meant by 'salvation.' Of course he was already fully saved, except that his body bore the marks of humiliation and suffering. It has been thought by some that he referred to his hope that his life might be preserved, and that release from captivity was not far away. In the Epistle to Philemon, which was written from Rome at the time of the writing of this Epistle, he says, 'Prepare me also lodging, for I hope that through your prayers I shall be granted unto you.' But it seems better to think that he believed that the coming of our Lord depended upon the extension of the Gospel throughout the known world, and that, therefore, all the preaching of the Cross which disseminated the knowledge of the Gospel, brought nearer that day to which he so often refers as the day of Christ, when the topstone should be placed upon the edifice, and complete salvation would come, not to him only, but to all those who loved the appearing. This yields a

Phil. i. 19, 20

good sense to the passage. He rejoiced in the preaching of this hostile faction, because it made Christ better known, and in so far as men knew and accepted Him, the coming of His Kingdom was hastened, which meant peace, joy, deliverance, and perfect life. When that long expected day was inaugurated, the last remains of sin would be destroyed in his heart, and the body of his humiliation would be changed for a body in the likeness of Christ. In this sense the word 'salvation' is employed elsewhere—'He shall appear the second time without sin unto salvation.'

How often has God overruled the designs and deeds of evil men for the glory of His name, the success of His Kingdom, and the salvation of His saints. What they mean for evil He turns to good. The oppression of Pharaoh, as we have seen, secures the establishment of Israel in their own land. The persecution of the Sanhedrin forced the early Christians to become evangelists throughout the empire. The Pope's bull against Luther inaugurated modern Protestantism. The persecution of the Stuarts urged the Pilgrim Fathers to lay the foundations of the great commonwealth in the United States. Truth has again and again been brought to the scaffold, and wrong has swayed the sceptre, but God is ever standing within the shadow 'keeping watch upon His own.' Be of good cheer, lift up your heads, your redemption draweth nigh!

For Christ was being Magnified

Paul rejoiced also because Christ was being magnified. The word 'expectation' has in it the idea of the uplifted head (Luke xxi. 28), the outstretched neck (Rom. viii. 19). It is as when one stands on tiptoe, anxiously looking for the advent of an anticipated prosperous issue out of affliction. The expectation of creation which waits for the revelation of the sons of God, had its counterpart in the Apostle's experience as he craned his neck in intense hope and anticipation that the great purpose of his life would be realised in the magnifying of the Lord. Each morning, as he arose, his soul was stirred with passionate thought and ambition that the hours should be as full as possible with whatever might promote the glory of his Master. Whatever event happened, he always questioned how far it would enhance men's estimation of the Lord. He thought comparatively little of what befell himself in the various incidents of his life, so long as each one furnished an increment of glory to the Master who filled the entire horizon of his affections. **Phil. i. 19, 20**

In the original Greek, their prayer and the supply of the Holy Spirit are so classed together as to be practically one. It is as though the Apostle felt that if only his Philippian friends would unite in earnest intercession, there could be no doubt as to the response. For *them* to pray for the Holy Spirit would be equivalent to *his* reception of Him. There are some prayers, concerning the answer to which we cannot be sure, for they deal with matters which are outside the promises of God, but wherever we claim for ourselves or others, things which God has offered us in Christ, we may be sure that to ask is to have.

Prayer besought

Throughout the Epistles the Apostle is constantly

Phil. i. 19, 20

asking for the prayers of his fellow disciples. 'Brethren, pray for us,' occurs more than once. He bids them 'help together by prayer.' In that touching exhortation at the close of the Epistle to the Romans, he entreats them to strive together in their prayers for him that he might be delivered from his enemies, and might come to them with joy by the will of God ; and in the Epistle to Ephesus and, probably, to the other Asiatic churches, he bids the disciples to pray always with all prayer and supplication in the Spirit, watching thereunto with all perseverance and supplication for all saints, adding significantly, 'and for me.' It is hardly possible to over-estimate the value of prayer, when some kindred soul really unites itself with us, in our temptations, sorrows, and efforts in the service of Christ. Full often some special influx of faith, hope, and courage is due to the fact that God is moving someone who loves us to strong entreaty and intercession on our behalf. The angels visited Sodom, laid their hands on Lot, and led him forth because Abraham, yonder on the heights, was pleading with God that if there were ten righteous, He would not destroy the city, not knowing that God was more eager to save Sodom than he to pray for it.

'The Supply of the Spirit of Jesus Christ'

'The supply of the Spirit of Jesus Christ' is a most interesting phrase. The Apostle describes the Holy Spirit as pre-eminently 'the Spirit of Jesus Christ.' Elsewhere he speaks of Him 'as the Spirit of the Son,' 'as the Spirit of life in Christ Jesus,' 'as the Spirit of Jesus.' There is ample warrant for this. Our Lord was conceived of the Holy Ghost, anointed by the Spirit at the waters of Baptism, Phil. i. 19, 20 filled with the Spirit as He was led up to be tempted, wrought His miracles and spoke His words in the power of the Holy Spirit, yielded Himself to the Father in death by the power of the Eternal Spirit, and was raised from the dead on the third day by the Spirit of Holiness, who is pre-eminently the Author of Resurrection Life. During the forty days, it was 'through the Holy Spirit that He gave commandment to the apostles whom He had chosen.' In answer to His intercession, He received the Holy Spirit in Divine fulness into His risen and exalted nature, and throughout the Acts He is represented as communicating the Spirit to those who seek Him by faith. Throughout this dispensation our Lord is, so to speak, the depository or storehouse of the Holy Spirit. It need hardly be said that the Spirit is equally Eternal and Divine with the Father and the Son, but during the present age, in the Divine economy, He is specially communicated through the nature of the Risen Lord to all members of His mystical Body, the Church, and works through them upon the world. We may be thankful, indeed, that as the blood circulates between the heart and the most distant member of the body, so does the Spirit of God unite us with Christ our Master. We are one with Him ; the very thoughts and emotions that occupy Him are conveyed to us ; because He lives we live also, by the direct impartation of His life.

'Supply'

The word *supply* demands our attention. It occurs, with its kindred verb, several times in the New Testament. It contains a suggestion of the choir or

Phil. i. 19, 20

singing entertainment, which was supplied on public occasions by some wealthy citizen to grace a triumphal entry, or celebrate some auspicious anniversary. It stands for the free and spontaneous furnishing of that which enriches and quickens the lives of others. It is as though the Apostle felt, that in answer to the prayer for which he pleaded, there would be a constant impartation into his nature of that Divine Spirit whose entrance brings joy and strength.

It is an important question to ask how far we know that same Spirit, who enables sufferers to discover reasons for thankfulness in their afflictions, lifts us out of our private tribulation into the great current of adoration and praise which is ever flowing towards the Throne of the Lamb, turns anxieties and privations into fountains of blessing and salvation, and inspires the one consuming purpose that Jesus should be glorified whether by life or death.

How to feel as St Paul did

As we read these wonderful paragraphs, and see how eager the Apostle was for the 'greatening' of Jesus, we feel the infection of his spirit and long to be animated by the same passion. There is no way of catching its fire, except by studying and obeying the laws on which the Holy Spirit is supplied to saints still. Nor is it enough to be acquainted with the method of operation, we must assiduously obey them, being sure that the Holy Spirit is a Spirit of method and order, and that He will immediately respond to the feeblest appeal made for His succour.

Let the poor dweller beside the Nile make the smallest channel in the time of flood, and the responsive water will forthwith flow into his little garden plot; so if by obedience and faith the channel is open towards the Blessed Spirit, there can be no doubt that He will immediately fill the heart with His abundance; though the glad recipient of His bounty will not concentrate his thought upon the Spirit of Jesus Christ, but pass through Him to Jesus Christ Himself. Just as we do not specially dwell upon the light which is the medium between the sun and our earth, but through sunlight live in contact with the mighty sun and orb of day; so those that are fullest of the Holy Spirit are fullest of the glory of Christ, and are most eager that He should be magnified in their bodies, whether it be by life or by death.

Phil. i. 19, 20

6

WHETHER TO LIVE, OR TO DIE!

Philippians 1:21-26

For to me to live *is* Christ, and to die *is* gain.

But if I live in the flesh, this *is* the fruit of my labour: yet what I shall choose I wot not.

For I am in a strait betwixt two, having a desire to depart, and to be with Christ; which is far better:

Nevertheless to abide in the flesh *is* more needful for you.

And having this confidence, I know that I shall abide and continue with you all for your furtherance and joy of faith;

That your rejoicing may be more abundant in Jesus Christ for me by my coming to you again.

Phil. i. 21-26

Life and Death

Omit the words 'Christ' and 'gain' and you are reminded how very close life and death lie; they are separated only by a comma. Life is the vestibule of death, and death follows closely upon life. The little babe is born and dies; the flower opens and fades; the spring seems hardly to have unfurled herself in summer before the leaves begin to fall; you clasp the hand of your friend in vigorous life to-day, to-morrow you hear that he has passed beyond the confines of our world. Life and death, the systole and diastole, the beat and throb of the pulse, the swing of the pendulum hither and thither. Every man stands where that comma stands, between life and death; all men are balancing between the two.

Probably there is not a single man or woman—the

exceptions, at least, are very rare—that does not at some time of life count the gain of life against death; and there is the balance on one side or the other, and sometimes the equilibrium. Now life is the heavier, and again death. So Hamlet and Paul may be compared, as representing two classes of men. There is the one class, represented by Hamlet, who weigh the *evils* of life and death; there are other men, like St Paul, who weigh the *blessings*. **Phil. i. 21-26**

Hamlet weighs the sorrows of life, from which death would relieve him, against the terrors of death, from which life delivers him. 'To be, or not to be, that is the question.' There are the sorrows of life, the whips and scorns of time, the rich man's pride, the proud man's contumely; and as he weighs these up upon the scale, he thinks that probably it would be better to die to escape them; but when he considers what death might bring, what dreams might come in death's sleep, he turns back to life as after all to be preferred.

St Paul, on the other hand, is impressed with the riches of life and death. He does not know which to choose, because each is so sweet. Life is sweet, because it is Christ; death is sweet, because it is more of Christ. And so he balances the one against the other, and presently exclaims: 'I am in a strait between the two. I do not know which of them to choose, but on the whole death preponderates, death is gain, to depart is far better.' So that we have just these two thoughts—the blessings of life, and the blessings of death, as regarded by the Apostle Paul.

The Epistle to the Philippians

Phil. i. 21-26
The Blessings of Life

'To me to live is Christ.' We may picture the Apostle Paul landing on the quay at Neapolis, the port of Philippi. His dress betokens travel and toil. Evidently a poor and somewhat insignificant man, unattended save by two or three as poor as himself. As he lands upon the busy quay he encounters many different men. There, for instance, is the merchant receiving his wares from the Orient, and preparing them for transit; he cries: 'To me to live is *wealth.*' Near him are the men who carry the packages from the ships to the emporiums of trade, or the great warehouses—the poor slaves—for them to live is *toil and suffering,* heavy blows and privations. Beside stands the philosopher, in his hand the scroll with the mystic words of wide knowledge, and as he looks upon the toil of the trader he prides himself that he lives for a superior aim, as he says: 'To me to live is *knowledge.*' Near to the little group is a soldier, who looks with contempt upon the man of letters, and cries: 'To me to live is *fame.*' Then the shadow of Octavius, the mighty emperor, who not far from Philippi won the great battle that gave him the empire of the known world, seems to rise amongst the group, crying in awful accents: 'To me to live is *empire.*' Amid all these voices the affirmation of the Apostle strikes in: 'To me to live is not wealth, nor hard work, nor literature, nor fame, nor glory, but *Christ.* Christ first, last, midst, all in all, and perpetually Christ.'

Christ—The Origin of our Life

If you had asked the Apostle just what he meant, he would probably have replied, as William Tyndale brings out in his translation, that Christ must be the *origin of our life.* The Day of Pentecost meant that from that moment, and onward, the Holy Spirit should bring the germ of the Christ-life, and sow it in the soil of our spirits, so that the very nature of Jesus glorified, transfigured and Divine, might be sown in the soil of our humanity, as incorruptible seed, to reproduce in endless succession the growth of the Christ-life. **Phil. i. 21-26**

The Essence of our Life

Christ must be the essence of our life. As we reckon ourselves dead to our own selfish existence, Jesus Christ will take its place, so that we may be able to exclaim with the Apostle : 'I live, yet not I, but Christ liveth in me.'

The Model of our Life

Christ must also be the model of our life. Every man works to a model. Consciously or unconsciously, we are always imitating somebody ; and every true Christian will endeavour, in ever-growing perfectness, to approximate to the measure of the stature of his Lord. 'It is enough that the disciple should be as His master.'

The Aim of our Life

Christ must also be the aim of our life. We desire to make Him known, loved, and revered, that His will may be done on earth as it is done in Heaven ; that others may know Him as we know Him, love Him as we love Him, live for Him as we live for Him ; that He may be the crowned King of men, putting down war and strife, and hastening on that glorious consummation, for which the Church prays and creation groans.

The Solace of our Life

Christ must be the solace of our life. Amid all the storm, strife, and tumult, there is no cleft where the Christian finds safe abiding, but in the riven

Phil. i. 21-26

Rock of Ages, in the side of the pierced Christ, in the heart of the Redeemer, the doors of which always stand open, and He is evermore bidding us come to Him for rest.

The Reward of our Life

Christ must be the reward of our life. The one reward for every Christian man is to get more of Christ; the one crown for every brow is to know Him better; the one infinite gain that comes for every labour, every tear, every act of sacrifice, is that Christ gives Himself, nearer, dearer, better than ever.

This enabled the Apostle, and enables us, to say, 'Life is good; it is worth living.' To live down here for Christ, to live in fellowship with Christ is to have the key to nature, to beauty, to love, to everything that is true and good. Life with all its darkness and sorrow is, after all, a good thing when a man can say, 'To me to live is Christ.'

* * *

The Blessings of Death

But 'to die is gain.' What are the blessings to which death introduces us? Let us weigh them up. First, *death is a beginning.* The world says it is an end; Scripture says it is the beginning of an endless series. Take, for instance, the term employed by the Apostle Peter. He spake of his *exodus*, 'his going out.' As the exodus was the beginning of the national life of Israel, their going out into freedom, so death is the exodus of the spirit into the freedom of eternity. The Apostle Paul speaks of death as *a birth*: 'The first-born from the dead.' It is the emergence of the spirit from the cramped, confined conditions of the first stage of its being into its true

Death a Birth

existence. He also speaks, in this passage, of death as a *loosing*. 'Having a desire to depart.' The Greek word there is marvellously beautiful; it is the unmooring of a vessel from its anchorage. We sometimes sing of the close of life thus:— **Phil. i. 21-26**

'Safe home, safe home in port!
 Rent cordage, shattered deck,
Torn sails, provisions short,
 And only not a wreck.'

How much truer is the conception suggested by Tennyson's description of the death of Arthur:—

'So said he, and the barge with oar and sail
Moved from the brink, like some full-breasted swan,
That, fluting a wild carol ere her death,
Ruffles her pure cold plume and takes the flood,
With swarthy webs.'

Death is Freedom

Secondly, *in death we become free.* It is the freeing of an imprisoned spirit: 'We that are in this tabernacle do groan being burdened, not that we would be unclothed, but clothed upon, that mortality might be swallowed up of life.' It is freedom from sin, freedom from the limitations of mortality, freedom from temptation, sorrow, care, and the anticipation and natural shrinking from death itself.

Death reveals Self

Thirdly, *death teaches us to discover our true selves.* You remember Rudyard Kipling's poem about the ship that thought she was a lump of rivets and iron; but after a while she was loosed, and glided out to the ocean to be tested by the storm and the tempest. But it was only as the winds screamed through her cordage, and every timber was strained, that she suddenly discovered that she was a ship. And so we

Phil. i. 21-26

do not know what we are, until we are loosed, until our nature, which is full of strange yearnings and discontent, finds its real consummation and bliss in eternity.

In death also the Christian who has lived Christ here passes through the veil and sees Christ. He is with Christ in a sense in which we cannot be with Him here. Here we walk by faith, there by sight, and we shall see His face, and His name shall be in our foreheads.

After Death with Christ

We can have no sympathy with the idea of some people who suppose that when we die we go into a kind of swoon, and stop there until the Judgment. Paul says: 'I shall see Christ, I shall be with Christ; for me to live is Christ, to die is gain, for I shall be with Christ, which is far better.' To be asleep would not be far better. If there is in reserve for us an experience far better than to live with Christ down here, it cannot be a negation, it must consist in more of Christ: nothing less would compensate the soul. When the spirit leaves for a little while the body which has been its humble friend, its companion and vehicle, laying it aside for a moment to take it again one day in transfigured beauty, it passes immediately into the presence of Jesus Christ, where it knows Him as it is known, and sees Him face to face.

And so far better

This seems something of what Paul meant when he said that death was gain. There was the beginning of the real life; there was the liberation, the emancipation of his life, so that it might find itself in the presence of Christ, and in Christ the recovery of all beloved ones that had gone before. Probably they are with us now by their sympathy, their prayer, their thought of us. But we have to be with Him before we can be literally with them. When you find Christ you will find all your loved ones again in Him. Bret Harte, in a poem quoted in this connection by Dr. Campbell Morgan, says:— Phil. i. 21-26

'As I stand by the Cross, on the lone mountain's crest,
Looking over the ultimate sea,
In the gloom of the mountain a ship lies at rest,
And one sails away from the lea;
One spreads its white wings on the far-reaching track,
With pennant and sheet flowing free;
One hides in the shadow with sails laid a-back,
The ship that is waiting for me.

But lo! in the distance the clouds break away,
The gate's glowing portals I see,
And I hear from the outgoing ship in the bay
The song of the sailors in glee.
So I think of the luminous footprints that bore
The comfort o'er dark Galilee,
And wait for the signal to go to the shore
To the ship that is waiting for me.'

Do you catch that thought? Two ships lying against the shore; one ship speeding out to sea in sunlight, the other ship waiting. That is your friend who has gone to Heaven, your wife, your child; this is your ship waiting for you. Some day you shall embark on that ship, the ship that is waiting for you. Mind that when that moment comes for loosing the shore-rope, you are ready.

* * *

Phil. i. 21-26

The Choice between the two.

'Nevertheless to abide in the flesh is more needful for you.' It is blessed to go when the Gate Beautiful opens to us, but there are reasons why the balance of choice may fall for the prolongation of life here. Granted that we shall know Christ there, *yet here we may know Him as the angels cannot.* They have never been tempted, have never fallen into sin, have never been solaced and comforted as we have been, have never continued with Him in all His trials and temptations, have never known Him forgiving sin with unwearied tenderness and pity, and lifting from the gates of death.

Life's Opportunities

Granted that we may serve Him yonder, yet we can hardly do such work for Him there as here. Tears do not need to be wiped in that fair world. Words of comfort are devoid of meaning. There are no prodigals to come home, no backsliders to be restored, no lost sheep to be sought.

The Privilege of Suffering

It is a good thing also to live for Christ here, *because we have the opportunity of suffering for Him.* Only here can we be nailed to His Cross, bear some of His shame, share our proportion of the blasphemy which is hurled upon His blessed person, or be reproached with His reproaches. Shakespeare makes King Henry say upon the field of Agincourt:

> 'For he to-day that sheds his blood with me
> Shall be my brother; be he ne'er so vile,
> This day shall gentle his condition:
> And gentlemen in England now abed
> Shall think themselves accursed they were not here.

So surely those who are beyond the reach of the pain

and trouble of this world,—babes like flowers nipped in early infancy,—will for ever be the losers because they never had the chance, as we have had, of standing alongside of Jesus Christ in this great battle. Phil. i. 21-26

The Privilege of Helping Others

It is also good to live in this world as long as we may, *because of the opportunities of helping others.* When a man thinks it quietly over, however great his longing it may be, to be gone, he reasons thus with himself: 'I can do good while I stay. I would like to be away, but there are downtrodden ones I may uplift, there are weaklings who want my help, there are lost ones to be saved, and for their sake I cannot wish to be gone before my time. Let me remain as a pilot at his wheel, as the shepherd near his flock, as a sentry at his post, as long as I can help one other soul.'

Often there come glimpses of the city; often there are love tokens thrown over its walls; often bunches of the everlasting flowers fall at our feet; often there are quaffs of the water of life; often the heavenly ones come and walk beside us, and speak of things in words that we cannot possibly reproduce. There are high moments in our life when the tide rises, when the chalice of our joy is full; but we turn back from the radiancy of glory, and the joys beyond compare, glad to abide in the flesh as long as there is one more lesson to learn, one more errand to fulfil, one more thirsty soul to refresh, one more backslider to bring home.

As His Lord did, so His great Apostle turned His back on the open door of Paradise, descended from

Phil. i. 21-26

the Transfiguration Mount, and set His face steadfastly to bear the Cross for a little longer. To abide in the flesh was manifestly better for these Philippian disciples especially, and indeed for many others in all the Churches, which Paul had been the means of founding; and there was borne in upon his mind the conviction that his willinghood to wait was accepted. 'Having this confidence,' he said—'the confidence that I can help you best by remaining with you—I know that I shall abide, and continue with you all for your progress and joy in the faith, that your rejoicing may be more abundant in Jesus Christ for me, by my coming to you again.' Not yet the final appearance before Nero: not yet the death-sentence: not yet the beheading beyond the city gate! A brief respite would be granted in which he would be able to pay another and farewell visit! One more meeting and parting, one more coming in and going out, one more Welcome and Good-bye. So the Lord had chosen for him, and so they required his help. He was therefore willing to turn back from the opened Heaven, with the immediate gain of death, to a few more tears, toils, and conflicts ere He should realise that the time of departure had really come (2 Tim. iv. 6, 7).

7

THE MANNER OF LIFE WHICH BECOMES THE GOSPEL

Philippians 1:27-30

ONLY let your conversation be as it becometh the gospel of Christ: that whether I come and see you, or else be absent, I may hear of your affairs, that ye stand fast in one spirit, with one mind striving together for the faith of the gospel;

And in nothing terrified by your adversaries: which is to them an evident token of perdition, but to you of salvation, and that of God.

For unto you it is given in the behalf of Christ, not only to believe on Him, but also to suffer for His sake;

Having the same conflict which ye saw in me, and now hear *to be* in me.

Phil. i. 27-30

A time of suspense

THE Apostle had been in suspense; on the one hand, the supreme interest of living was that he might know and serve Christ; on the other hand, to die would be gain because it would usher him into an existence with wider horizons and opportunities. Which of the two to choose had thrown him into difficulty and suspense. Finally, however, he had come to the conclusion, that, in all probability, the hour for striking his tent, weighing his anchor, and departing to be with Christ had not come, and that he would have still to abide in the flesh, staying at his post, maintaining his witness on behalf of the Gospel, and bearing the burden and weight of the

Phil. i. 27-30

Churches which looked to him as their father. As far as he was concerned, it was infinitely better to go to be with Christ, but for the sake of the work that needed him, he realised that it was more necessary to remain with his fellow-believers, as their comrade and helper, so as to promote their progress in the knowledge of God, and their joy in believing.

How to live meanwhile

He counted, therefore, with almost absolute certainty that he would return again to Philippi, and already he seemed to hear their shouts of rejoicing as he disembarked at the quay, and was welcomed by the membership of the Church which had come down to Neapolis to greet him. In order that that glad hour might be a sky without clouds, that there might be nothing to jar on the greatness of their mutual gladness, he urged that their conversation (lit. their citizenship) should be worthy of the Gospel of Christ, so that whether he came to see them or was compelled still to be absent, he might hear good tidings of their steadfastness, unity, undaunted courage, and willingness to suffer.

Our 'Conversation'

The word *conversation* is the rendering of a Greek word, which is familiar to us in the terms 'police,' 'politics,' 'politicians.' Its primary reference is to cities and city life. The Apostle thought of the Philippian disciples as citizens. They were citizens of Rome in the first instance, but they were also citizens of the Heavenly Jerusalem. Later on in this Epistle he says, 'Our conversation (lit. citizenship) is in heaven.' Is not this true of us all? Much as we glory in our earthly citizenship, we have more to glory in when we remember that we are under a Divine Sovereign, that we owe allegiance to Heavenly laws, and that we have burgess rights in the City of God. This, Macaulay tells us, in his eloquent description of the Puritans, was their pride and boast, and it may be ours. We desire a better country, that is, an heavenly, and believe that God has prepared for us a city. We confess that we are pilgrims and strangers on the earth, because we greet from afar the Celestial City, the home of God's elect.

The word, in the course of usage, obtained a wider significance than citizenship, and refers to the manner of life which is incumbent on all those, who by faith have become children of the Jerusalem which is above. We have daily to live in a manner which becomes our high calling and great profession.

We must be Steadfast

'That ye stand fast.' It is comparatively easy to mount up with wings, to run without wearying, and even to walk without fainting, but the hardest matter is to stand fast. Not going back, not yielding to the pressure of circumstances, not cowering before the foe, but quietly, resolutely, and determinedly holding our ground. This note rings through the Apostle's writings. 'Having done all,' he cries, 'see that ye withstand in the evil day, and stand' (Eph. vi. 13, 14). In this Epistle, we shall find him bidding his brethren 'stand fast in the Lord' (iv. 1). Evidently, in his judgment, steadfastness was of supreme importance in the make-up of character.

It is good to begin, but it is better to keep on

Phil. i. 27-30

steadily to the end. It is much when the young soldier, well equipped for battle, steps out into the early dawn, with the light shining upon his weapons, but it is more important far, if, in the late afternoon, he is found standing in the long thin line, resisting the perpetual onset of the foe. We are told of Daniel, that he 'continued' (Dan. i. 21). This, perhaps, is the greatest tribute to him, that through decades he did not swerve from his loyalty to God, or devotion to the high interests which were committed to his charge. The men that are steadfast in their loyalty to truth, in their prosecution of duty, in their holding the post assigned to them by the providence of God, are those which leave the deepest impression on their contemporaries. It is not the flash of the meteor which the world really wants, but the constant radiance of the fixed star. What though the storm beats in your face, and every effort is made to dislodge you, though it seems as if you were forgotten in that lone post of duty, still stand fast: the whole situation may depend upon your tenacity of purpose, the campaign may be decided by your holding your ground without flinching. If the Master has put you as a light on the cellar stair, never desert that post because it is lonely and distasteful, and because the opportunity of service comes rarely. To be found doing your duty at the unexpected moment, when His footfall is heard along the corridor, will be a reward for years of patient waiting.

We must preserve the Spirit of Unity

'In one spirit, with one mind (R.V. *soul*) striving together (lit. wrestling) for the faith of the Gospel.'

The Life which becomes the Gospel

The idea of the Apostle is derived from the ancient games, when men might wrestle side by side against those of another city or nation. We put each other in good heart when we stand and strive shoulder to shoulder. The regiments which are drawn from the same locality, are most likely to give a good account of themselves in the battle. Every care should be taken to guard against the outbreak of misunderstanding and jealousy, for these, more than anything else, will induce a spirit of disunion, which is the sure precursor of failure. **Phil. i. 27-30**

In the Home

To use the illustration of our Lord, the homes that are united are irresistible in their impact upon men, the household which is divided against itself cannot stand. So it is with the alliances, leagues, and parties of human politics; so it is with the army, with federations of operatives, or in the administration of the affairs of state. Directly there are suspicions, jealousies, envies; so soon as men are alienated by the spirit of faction and intrigue; directly parties are for themselves rather than for the state;—paralysis ensues.

In the Church

In Church life, it is of course necessary that each should preserve his individuality. Each stone in the foundation of the New Jerusalem must flash with its own lustre. Each star must shine with its own glory; each ray in the prism must be itself, or the pure beam of light cannot be produced. The very glory of our common Church life is in the play and mutual interaction of different temperaments, dispositions, and character. A dull uniformity is much to be feared. 'If the different members of

Phil. i. 27-30

each Church were similar, if all held the same views, all spoke the same words, all viewed truth from the same stand-point, they would have no unity, but would be simply an aggregate of atoms —the sand pit over again.' But amid all these differences there may be a true unity, the different notes may make one splendid burst of music, the different regiments may be animated by a common heroism, the crowd of Medes, Parthians, Elamites, Mesopotamians, Cretans and Arabians, Jews and Gentiles, may make one Church, of whom it may be said 'They continued with one accord in the temple, and in breaking bread at home.' Whatever we do as members of Christian organisations, we should lay stress upon the things in which we are agreed, and refuse to be alienated over inconsiderable matters, about which we differ.

We must show Courage in the Presence of our Enemies

'In nothing affrighted by the adversaries, which is to them an evident token of perdition, but to you of salvation, and that from God.' The adversaries include the virulent hate of Jews who dogged the footsteps of the Apostle, and sought to overthrow his work, and the strong hatred of the Gentiles, which showed itself in the cruel scourging and imprisonment to which Paul and Silas had been subjected ten years before. The origin of the word translated *affrighted,* suggests the behaviour of a horse when it becomes scared, springs aside, or dashes off wildly. It is an expression of panic and dismay; as if one should say, 'It is vain to resist, the enemy is too strong.'

In point of fact, our adversaries bluster much, but

effect very little. They come near to us, as Goliath to David, threatening the terrible things that they are prepared to perpetrate for our undoing, but when they discover that we manfully hold our own, they recoil as the waves from the rocks and cliffs of the shore. It seems, sometimes, as though the ocean would prevail, the mighty waves, mountain high, come towering towards the coast, but within a moment there is nothing to show for their fury but a mass of foam. It was so with the Spanish Armada, when with loud defiance it was hurled against Elizabeth; it was so with the long strife that followed the burning of John Huss and Jerome at Prague, when all Europe arrayed itself against their followers in vain. 'Lo the kings assemble themselves, they pass away together; they saw it and then were they amazed; they were dismayed and were stricken with terror; trembling took hold of them there, and pain as of a woman in travail; with the east wind Thou breakest the ships of Tarshish.'

Phil. i. 27-30

Courage becomes God's servant

Undaunted courage becomes the servant of God. It shone in the faces of the three young men, who told the king that they would not bow down to his graven image. It inspired the apostles, who told the Sanhedrin that they must obey God rather than men. It flamed forth in Luther's lonely stand against the papacy. 'Be of good comfort, Master Ridley,' said Latimer, 'and play the man, we shall this day light such a candle, by God's grace, in England, as I trust shall never be put out.' In these words was evidence of the undaunted courage

Phil. i. 27-30

which has never failed to animate the martyrs of Jesus. It is impossible to ordinary flesh and blood, but, by faith, we may receive the lion-heart of Him, who is not only the Lamb as it had been slain, but the Lion of the tribe of Judah.

We must accept Suffering as a Gift from God

'To you it hath been granted in the behalf of Christ, not only to believe on Him, but also to suffer in His behalf; having the same conflict which ye saw in me, and now hear to be in me.' How greatly these words must have encouraged the Philippian Christians! They realised that the Apostle looked upon them as fellow soldiers in the same fight as that in which for a life-time he had been engaged. Their steadfastness and victory at Philippi would make his own resistance easier, just as his heroism in Rome sent a thrill of courage and hope into that far distant city. They were comrades, fellow soldiers, entrusted with similar responsibility on behalf of the dear Lord who was leading the fight.

Our Victories are our Lord's

The same thought was in the mind of the Master, when, on the return of the seventy from casting out a few demons, He said, 'I beheld Satan fallen as lightning from heaven.' He encouraged them by reminding them that their victories were His. So is it always. There is not a single lad at whom shoes are thrown in the bedroom by his school-fellows, because he says his prayers beside his bed; there is not a girl who brings on herself the derisive epithets of her fellow factory hands, because she reads her Testament in the dinner hour; there is not a single working man who endures obloquy and reproach, the hiding of his tools, and exclusion from the companionship of his fellow workmen, because he dares to rebuke their blasphemous and impure conversation, who is not sharing in that same conflict, which is always raging between heaven and hell.

Phil. i. 27-30

Suffering for Christ's Sake is a Gift

In that conflict suffering is inevitable, but let us dare to recognise that suffering for Christ's sake is a gift. 'It is *given* to you on behalf of Christ.' He entrusts money to some, learning to others, gifts of speech and organisation to others, but to some, who may well stand in the inner circle, He gives the prerogative to suffer. Accept your suffering as a precious gift from His hand, and dare to believe that in and through it all, you are filling up that which is behind of His own suffering, for His Body's sake, which is the Church. You are being admitted into His Gethsemane to watch with Him, your suffering is precious in His sight, and will have a distinct and undoubted effect in hastening the advent of His Kingdom.

8

THE ENTWINING OF CHRISTIAN HEARTS

Philippians 2:1-4

IF *there be* therefore any consolation in Christ, if any comfort of love, if any fellowship of the Spirit, if any bowels and mercies,

Fulfil ye my joy, that ye be like-minded, having the same love, *being* of one accord, of one mind.

Let nothing *be done* through strife or vainglory; but in lowliness of mind let each esteem other better than themselves.

Look not every man on his own things, but every man also on the things of others.

Phil. ii. 1-4

Fellowship is essential to growth of character

FELLOWSHIP is essential to the true development of character. Ever since the Creation it has not been good for man to be alone. *The Swiss Family Robinson* was always more interesting to me than *Robinson Crusoe,* because the latter was alone on the island, whilst the former was a family group. No man can be satisfied to live by himself. It may be necessary, but he will not attain his full growth. He needs fellowship with those above him, with those beside him, and with those below him, in order to attain his full maturity.

Such Fellowship is Communion

Such fellowship must be inward rather than outward. It must be communion rather than communication; it must be in spirit and sympathy more than in outward form. If a man is only conscious that he is in sympathy with kindred souls he does not so much mind if they be silent. If there be at this moment some noble angel who has been commissioned by the Almighty to undertake a distant errand to one of the environs of the universe, and who at this moment is plying his mighty flight through ether, intent on executing the purpose of the Most High, his noble bosom heaving with adoration, devotion, and praise, even though his back should be turned to the metropolis of the universe from which he has started, in those distant seas of space, from which no answering angel voice responds to his, and where his voice alone awakens the echoes with the praise of the Eternal, he probably is not conscious of solitude, or loneliness, or isolation, because his heart is beating in sympathy with the great host of beings he has left behind him. It is not necessary, therefore, that we should have outward contact with people to derive the development of character, which comes from sympathy; if the contact is inner and heart to heart, it is enough for the achieving of the Divine purpose. **Phil. ii. 1-4**

It must come through a Common Medium

This fellowship will best come to us through a common medium. Of course, there are many cases of affinity in which man is drawn to man, and woman to woman, and man to woman, by a sort of inward attraction and approximation of heart to heart. But this is not so strong for the most part as their common adherence to a common interest. There may be the aggregation of sand-grains, which have been moistened and compressed until they appear to cohere, but directly they become dry they disintegrate and fall apart, atom from atom; whereas, supposing a number of grains of iron dust to accumulate around a common magnet, because the iron attracts them to

Phil. ii. 1-4

itself it attracts them also to one another, and there is no disintegration, but a perpetual welding. So it is with groups of men. Men may be pressed together from without, whose union is but temporary. But again, other men may embrace one common principle, and become compacted into a cohesive whole. For the most part it is better, therefore, for us to adhere to one another because of their adhesion to a common centre or medium.

The Medium may be a Common Sentiment

This knitting medium may be a common sentiment. For instance, take the children of a home—a brother and sister. Their spirits came, God alone knows whence, but they met together in this common family circle. The common life of the father, of the mother, of the dear old ancestral residence, of the antique furniture, of the garden, or farm,—these create the common sentiments that yield for those two a medium of unusual attractiveness. So it is with two artists. Their common interest in the beautiful, that they catch bewitching nature in her shyest moods, that they are students together of the secrets of creation—these common sentiments will draw them together. They may have met in some little village, never having known each other before, but from that week which they spend together, they become welded by a common sentiment. So it is with two reformers, men who have come from different parts of England, who speak different dialects of English; they meet in a common council chamber, hear some great programme unfolded, and leap to their feet with enthusiastic acclamation. Then, as they leave the hall by the same staircase, talking casually, the two men find themselves drawn together; and from that moment a tie is wrought between them which will unite them like Cobden and Bright—brothers for the remainder of their existence.

Phil. ii. 1-4

Better still, a Common Devotion

Higher and better than the adhesion to a sentiment is a common devotion to a person. That is what made the unity of the Cave of Adullam. David's followers had come from all parts of Israel; they were, many of them, men of rude and rough character; some were debtors, some outlaws; but as soon as they reached that spot and gathered around the magnetic personality of David, they became consolidated into a fellowship, before the impact of which the kingdom of Saul fell. He could not resist the mighty impulse of that united band of brothers, that gathered each to the other, because they gathered around David. And in our own English story, what made the unity of the Table Round, which drove out the heathen and righted wrong throughout the whole country, except the fact that King Arthur was there, the leader, the prince, the centre, in whom each of the units found union and cohesion with every other?

What is it that makes the British Empire? Is it not because distant colonies, countries, cities, and vast extended territories find their centre of unity in the personality of the Sovereign? In the old village life of England, the fact that men, women, and children came for water to the common well, that stood in the centre of the village green, made the whole village become one by its common attraction to that moss-grown well.

Phil. ii. 1-4

Best of All: God the Medium

It is best of all when that medium is God Himself.—God in the person of Christ. You can see that in a minute, if you have noticed the change that comes over a family when religion enters it. Before religion came the father, mother, and children were bound by a certain bond to each other; there were no jars, no jealousy, no strife; but when a revival comes over the Church, and the larger number, if not all, in the household become truly regenerate, there is a new depth, a new blessedness in the family life. God is in the meals, God is in the play and recreation; the thought of God persuades and permeates the whole house. The presence of God gives a new meaning to every affection, pursuit, engagement, and faculty—a new wealth and beauty pour into them all.

Two men may have been drawn to each other by a common sentiment. After a while they become religious, each begins to love God. They love one another better, touch one another at deeper points, become in every way more to one another. Those two men have taken the bulb of friendship, which could hardly thrive in the cold atmosphere to which it was exposed, and have planted it amid the kindly atmosphere of the love of God, and the poor sickly plant has unfurled a fragrance and beauty of colour which had never before been possible. So you see, however great the drawings we have to one another on the same and lower platform of common interests or sentiments towards a given centre, there is no such fellowship as that which is born in us when we are welded together in a common love to Jesus Christ and a common devotion to the interests of His kingdom. This is the basis of closest fellowship, when our souls are bound together by a strong deep attachment to God in Christ. Phil. ii. 1-4

* * *

According to this passage there are five bonds of union and fellowship in the Gospel.

Bonds of Union: Consolation

The first bond is the *consolation which is in Christ.* For *consolation* let us substitute *exhortation,* or, better still, *persuasiveness,* so that we might put it that the first bond of Christian fellowship is Christ's persuasiveness. That Jesus Christ is interested in every Church fellowship is obvious, but we do not always realise how much He is always doing to *persuade* us to maintain it. Have there not been times in your life when you have been greatly incensed, but have realised that there was a voice speaking within your heart, and a gentle influence stealing over you, a yearning towards the brother about whom you had cherished hard and unkind feelings? That has been the persuasiveness of Christ. It is He who has besought you to check that word, to refrain from writing that letter, to abandon that bitter and offensive way which had seemed so befitting a method of repaying your enemy to his face. It was Christ who was persuading you to drop the weapon from your hand, and to reach it out in brotherhood, and this because He was so eager to keep the unity of the Spirit unbroken in the bond of peace.

The Comfort of Love

The second bond is the *comfort of love.* The Greek word will bear this rendering—*if you know the tender cheer that love gives;* that is, see to it

Phil. ii. 1-4

that you maintain the bond of Christian fellowship by meeting your fellow Christians with the tender cheer of love. We all know what tender cheer is, when men have been out all day and tried, almost beyond endurance. As they come out of the storm, the depression of their spirit and their health may have conspired to reduce them to the lowest depth of darkness—then as the door opens, and they see the ruddy glow of the fire, and the wife comes to meet them, and the child is there with its prattle, for a moment it seems almost worth while having known the weariness and depression because of the contrasted cheer that greets them. All around us in the world are Christian hearts which are losing faith; many hands hang down, and knees shake together. Let us see to it that by the kindly cheer of a smile, the grasp of a hand, the welcome of a word, we do something to draw those people into the inner circle of Christian love.

The Fellowship of Spirit

The third bond is *the fellowship of the Spirit.* The word means *to share the Spirit,* the going in common with the Spirit. They who live near God know what that fellowship is; they know that they are always accompanied; that they are never for one moment by themselves; can never enter a room with the consciousness of vacancy; can never travel in an empty car with a sense of isolation and solitude: there is always the fellowship of the Spirit. Whatever any one man knows of this fellowship every other knows. Each Christian person is conscious of the same Presence, making evident and obvious to us the same Jesus Christ.

The same atmosphere is lighted by the same sun; and in proportion as we have fellowship with the same Spirit we cannot lose our temper with each other, or be hard, cross, and unkind. Phil. ii. 1-4

'Bowels of Mercies'

The fourth bond is, '*Bowels of mercies.*' The old Greek word stands for humanness aud pity. In the former clause we were called upon to manifest the kindly cheer, that welcomes the weary soldier on his return from the campaign, for equals of whose heart-sorrow we have some inkling; but now we are to show fellowship for our dependants and subordinates, for the fallen, the weak, the weary, for those whose spirits cry out in agony. And in acting thus we are doing what we can to co-operate with Christ in His consolation, and with the Holy Ghost in His fellowship, to build up and compact the Church into a living unity.

A Common Mind and Purpose

The fifth bond is *one common mind and purpose*—'That ye be like-minded, being of one accord and of one mind.' It recalls the sentence in the book of Chronicles which tells us that every day men came from all Israel with one mind to make David king. So the deepest thought in Christian fellowship, and that which makes us truly one, is the desire to make Jesus King, that He may be loved and honoured, that thousands of souls may bow the knee and confess that He is Lord. Oh! that this were ever the prominent thought among us.

In such an atmosphere, where all love one another and live for the common object of the glory of Jesus, three things follow:—

Three Results

(1) *Party spirit dies.*—'Let nothing be done through strife or partizanship.' One cannot say, I

Phil. ii. 1-4 am of Apollos; another, I am of Cephas; because all are of Christ.

(2) *There is absolute humility.* Each thinks the other better than himself. Why? Because each looks upon the best things in another and the worst things in himself; and it is only when you compare what you know yourself to be with what you think others are, that you become absolutely humble. By comparing what we sadly deplore in ourselves with what we admire in others it is not difficult to think everybody better than ourselves. Out of this there comes—

(3) *The habit is formed of looking upon other men's things and not upon our own.* We acquire a wide sympathy. When we know God we begin to see something of Him in people who have been accustomed to very different surroundings to ourselves. We realise that those who do not belong to our fold may yet belong to the same flock. When we love Christ best it is wonderful how soon we discover Him in people who do not belong to our Church, or denomination, or system, but who also love Him best, are living the same life, and filled with the same spirit. We never relax our loyalty to our special Church, but we enlarge our sympathy to embrace the great Church, the Body of Christ.

Perhaps you have not yet entered the life of love! You do not know what the love of God is—your sin has made you evil and selfish. But if you are willing to abandon your selfish, sinful life, and kneel at the foot of the Cross, asking for forgiveness and salvation, step by step you will enter that experience which we have been describing, and which is in this world as an oasis amid wastes of wilderness sand.

9

HE EMPTIED HIMSELF

Philippians 2:5-8

LET this mind be in you, which was also in Christ Jesus:
Who, being in the form of God, thought it not robbery to be equal with God:
But made Himself of no reputation, and took upon Him the form of a servant, and was made in the likeness of men:
And being found in fashion as a man, He humbled Himself, and became obedient unto death, even the death of the cross.

Phil. ii. 5-8

Majesty and Humility combined

IN the whole range of Scripture this paragraph stands in almost unapproachable and unexampled majesty. There is no passage where the extremes of our Saviour's majesty and humility are brought into such abrupt connection. Guided by the Spirit of God, the Apostle opens the golden compasses of his imagination and faith, and places the one point upon the supernal Throne of the eternal God, and the other upon the Cross of shame where Jesus died, and he shows us the great steps by which Jesus approached always nearer and nearer to human sin and need; that, having embraced us in our low estate, He might carry us back with Himself to the very bosom of God, and that by identifying Himself with our sin and sorrow He might ultimately identify us with the glory which He had with the Father before the world was. And this wonderful description of His descent to our shame and sorrow is here cited by the Apostle, that it might be a living

Phil. ii. 5-8

impulse and inspiration to ourselves, not to look upon our own things, not to hold them with a tight grasp, but to be willing to stoop for others to shame, sorrow, and spitting; fulfilling God's purpose of mercy to the world, even as Jesus Christ, who became the instrument and organ through which God's redemptive purpose wrought. 'Let this mind be in you.' Think these thoughts. Never look exclusively upon your own interests, never count anything of your own worthy to stand in the way, but always be prepared to the last point to deny yourself, that the redemptive purpose of God may flow through the channel of your life to those that sorely need His blessed help. It is a wonderful thing that, day by day, in our poor measure, we may repeat the purpose and the work of Jesus Christ our Emmanuel.

No rhetoric or metaphor of ours can add to the splendour of these words, but in the simplest possible way we will stand on these seven successive slabs of chrysolite.

* * *

Christ in the Form of God

First, HE WAS IN THE FORM OF GOD. The Greek word translated "form" means a great deal more than the external appearance; it stands for the essence of God's nature, so that we may say that Jesus Christ possessed the essence of the Divine quality and nature from all eternity. This exactly agrees with other words of Scripture, as when we are told, He is '*the image of the invisible God.*' Again, '*Being the effulgence of His glory,*' i.e. He was the outshining beam of the Father's glory; 'and the *very image of His substance,'* i.e. He corresponded to the Divine Nature, as a seal to the die. Again, '*The Word was with God, and the Word was God.*' '*All things were made by Him.*' And then, as we overhear that marvellous communion between the Son and the Father, in John xvii., we notice His reference to the glory He had with the Father before the worlds were made, and with which He asks the Father to glorify Him in His human nature again. All these deep words prove that whatever God was in the uncreated eternity of the past,—the infinite, the incomprehensible, the all-holy, and the all-blessed,—that was Jesus Christ, who was absolutely one with Him, as spirit and soul are one in the organisation of our nature. **Phil. ii. 5-8**

* * *

It was not Robbery

Secondly, THERE WAS NO ROBBERY WHEN HE CLAIMED EQUALITY WITH GOD. Indeed, as R.V. puts it, it was *not a thing to be grasped,* because He was so sure of it. It was conceded to Him universally; He counted it no robbery; He thought it detracted nothing from the Father's infinite glory when He stood on an equality with Him; and it is remarkable to notice how in the four courts of earthly life He prosecuted His claim. There are four courts for us all.

Four Courts

In the court of His intimates. On the highway to Cæsarea Philippi, He asked His disciples whom men took Him to be; and Peter cried, 'Thou art the Christ, the Son of the living God.' This could not have meant that the Lord Jesus was the Son as we are sons. That would have been a meaningless

Phil. ii. 5-8

response. There was something more than that. And Jesus took it to be more, because He said, 'Flesh and blood hath not revealed it unto thee, but My Father which is in heaven.' In those words He took to Himself the prerogative of equality with God. You remember how He said afterwards: 'Ye believe in God,'—give Me the same faith, 'believe also in Me.' He thought it not robbery to receive the faith that man gives to God. He said significantly: 'My Father and I,'—'*We* will come and make our abode with him.' He thought it not robbery to enter the human soul and to share its occupancy with the Father. With His intimates He always spoke of Himself as One with the Father, in an incomprehensible, mysterious, but essential oneness.

So also in the court of public opinion. He said, 'I and My Father are One,' with an emphasis that made the Jews catch up stones to cast at Him, because, being a man, He claimed to be God. And He also told them that all men were to honour the Son even as they honour the Father. He thought it not robbing God to accept the honour men gave to Him.

So also in the court of justice. We know how the priests challenged Him, and asked Him to declare His essential nature, and said, 'Art Thou the Son of the living God?'—using the word *son* in the sense the Jews always did use it, as intimating essential Deity; and He said, 'Thou sayest that I am: and hereafter ye shall see the Son of man coming in the glory of God,'—for He did not think it robbery to share God's prerogative and place.

Finally, in the court of death. When death came, and He hung upon that cross of agony, He did not for a moment retract all that He had said, but opened the gate to the dying thief, and assured him that he would be that day with Him in Paradise,—for He did not think it robbing God to assume the right of opening the gates of forgiveness and life. **Phil. ii. 5-8**

All through His earthly life He insisted upon it that He was God's equal, God's fellow, and that He was One with the Father.

* * *

He emptied Himself

Thirdly, HE EMPTIED HIMSELF. This was evidently by His free will and choice. He emptied Himself *of His glory.* As Moses veiled the glory that shone upon his face, so Emmanuel veiled the glory that irradiated from His Person. We are told they need no sun in heaven, because His Presence is sun. What an effulgence of light must have streamed from Jesus, the Second Person of the Holy Trinity, in those uncreated ages! But when He stepped down to earth He veiled it,—the Word became flesh and tabernacled among us,—the Shekinah nature was shrouded, so that it was not able to penetrate, save on the Mount of Transfiguration, when, for a moment, the voluntary act by which Christ hid His intrinsic splendour was laid aside, and it welled out in cascades and torrents of blinding light.

But probably we are specially here taught that He emptied Himself *of the use of His divine attributes.* This is a profound truth which it is necessary to understand if you would read rightly the lesson of our Saviour's life. Men have been accustomed to

Phil. ii. 5-8

think that the miracles of Jesus Christ were wrought by the putting forth of His intrinsic and original power as God: that when He hushed the storm, and the waves crouched like whelps to His feet,—that when He raised the dead, and Lazarus sheeted with grave-clothes came forth,—that when He touched the sight of the blind, and gave eyeballs to those that had been born without their optics,—that all this was done by the forthputting of His own original, uncreated, and divine power; whereas a truer understanding of His nature, specially as disclosed in the Gospel by St John, shows that He did nothing of Himself, but what He saw the Father doing; that the words He spoke were not His own words, but as He heard God speaking He spoke; that the works He did were not his own, but the Father's who sent Him, for when they said on one occasion 'Show us the Father,' He replied, 'He that hath seen Me hath seen the Father; the words I speak to you I speak not from Myself, but the Father that dwelleth in Me, He doeth His works.' His human life was one of faith, even as ours should be: 'As the living Father hath sent Me, and I live by the Father, even so he that eateth Me shall live by Me.' Frequently He paralleled our experience with His own; and no doubt the story of the Vine in which He depicts our dependence upon Himself, had long been in His thought as an emblem of His own dependence upon the Father. He chose to live like this. He voluntarily laid aside the exercise of His omnipotence, that He might receive power from God; absolutely and voluntarily forewent the use of attributes that lay all around Him, like tools within the reach of the skilled mechanic, that He might live a truly human life, weeping our tears, and receiving the plenitude of His Father's power. Phil. ii. 5-8

*   *   *

Christ in the Form of a Servant

Fourthly, HE TOOK UPON HIM THE FORM OF A SERVANT. The infinite God, with whom He was One, desired to achieve certain purposes in our world; and the blessed Christ, the Second Person in the Trinity, undertook to be the medium and vehicle through which the Father might express Himself: and just as the words that issue from our mouth are impressed with our intelligence—the liquid air around us yielding itself to the movements of the larynx, so that what is in our mind is communicated and conveyed to others as they listen—so Jesus Christ became the Word of God, impressed with the thought, mind, and intention of God, so that the Father was able, through the yielded nature of the Son, to do, say, and be everything He desired. Christ was the perfect expression of the Being of Him whom no man hath seen, or can see.

It is so absurd, therefore, to divorce Jesus from the Father. Preachers have made an awful mistake when they have spoken of the Atonement as though Jesus intervened to appease the Father, to satisfy something in God that needed satisfaction before He could love. On the contrary, the whole Bible substantiates the belief that God was in Christ; and that what Christ did, God did through Him, and that the death on the cross was the act of the entire Deity. What wonder, then, that the Father said,

Phil. ii. 5-8

'Behold My Servant whom I have chosen, Mine elect, in whom My soul is well pleased. I will put My Spirit upon Him, and He shall show judgment to the Gentiles.'

* * *

In the Likeness of Men

Fifthly, HE WAS MADE IN THE LIKENESS OF MEN. He must know what the experiences of a human body are, what childhood and boyhood, and what it is to pass through the various stages of manhood. It was needful that He should be as perfectly united with man as He was perfectly united with God, so that He might be made a merciful and faithful High Priest, to make intercession for our sins—for all these reasons—He did not abhor the Virgin's womb, but was made man. Let us not fear too much the mystery and burden of human life. Our Lord and Master has gone this way before us, and has left a track behind, as they who traverse the Australian bush break twigs or branches along their route, to serve as a guide to those who follow. It is good to be born, that we may have a share in the nature He has worn.

* * *

Christ obedient to Death

Sixthly, HE DIED. He need not have died, because He was sinless; and death was only the result of sin. Adam sinned, and so died; Jesus did not sin, and therefore needed not to pass through death's portal. From the Mount of Transfiguration, He might, had He chosen, have stepped back into heaven, as Adam might have been caught back to God, if he had not eaten of the forbidden fruit. Had our first parents not yielded to temptation, our race would still have peopled the world, and would have passed away, as, at the Second Advent, those will, who are alive and remain,—suddenly changed, not seeing death, and their mortality swallowed up of life. From the Mount of Transfiguration Jesus Christ could have stepped into heaven, His body passing in a moment, in the twinkling of an eye, through its supreme transfiguration. But, had this been the case, He would never have made the reparation due to the holy law which man had broken. And therefore, with calm deliberation, and with full knowledge of all that awaited Him, He came down the mountain-side, and yielded Himself to death. He laid down His life at the cross, and bowed His meek head beneath death's sceptre. He had power to lay down His life, as a voluntary gift and sacrifice for our race ; and He used it. Though Lord of all, He became obedient to the last dread exaction of human penalty: and, through death, destroyed him that had the power of death. **Phil. ii. 5-8**

* * *

Even the Death of the Cross

Seventhly, HE CHOSE THE MOST DEGRADING AND PAINFUL FORM OF DEATH. There were several methods of death—by decapitation, by the stoppage of the heart's action, or by drinking poison. The death of the cross was the death of the slave, the most shameful and ignominious. Cicero said that it was far, not only from the bodies but the imagination of Romans. Therefore, since this death was the most shameful through the exposure of the person, the most degrading, the most painful known to man, the Saviour chose it. He could not have gone any lower.

Phil. ii. 5-8

One has sometimes imagined how He might have died—in the home of Bethany, with the window open towards Jerusalem, Mary wiping the death-dew from His brow, and Martha waiting on His every need, whilst Lazarus gave Him a brother's help. But this could not be the Lord's choice, in view of the fact that He must taste death for every man, and be made a curse, and be able to put His everlasting arms beneath those of His followers, who have died the most excruciating and shameful deaths.

That Mind must be in us

We must be willing to lay aside our ambition and glory, our thrones of comfort, respect, and power, if by doing so we may be the better able to succour others. We must be willing to take the form of servants, to wash one another's feet, to submit even to shame and spitting, to misunderstanding and opprobrium, if we shall thereby help to lift the world nearer God. There is no other way of sitting with Jesus on His throne, no other method by which we may assist Him, however feebly, in His work of saving others. There are plenty among us like the two brethren who would sit right and left in the Kingdom, who will never be able to attain thereto because they will not pay the price of drinking His cup and being baptised with His baptism. They will not take the low seat, or stoop to the obscure and unnoticed tasks: they love the honour that comes from human applause, and the notoriety which accrues from conspicuous notices in the daily press. God help and forgive us for yielding to these insidious temptations, and give us the Spirit of our Lord, that the same mind may be in us as in Him.

He emptied Himself

Kepler, when he first turned his telescope to resolve Phil. ii.
the nebulæ, said, 'I am thinking over again the 5-8
first thoughts of God'; but surely it is given to us to think still earlier thoughts than those of Creation, even those which were in the heart of the Lamb who was slain in the Divine Purpose before the worlds were framed.

10

THE NAME OF NAMES

Philippians 2:9-11

WHEREFORE God also hath highly exalted Him, and given Him a name which is above every name:

That at the name of Jesus every knee should bow, of *things* in heaven, and *things* in earth, and *things* under the earth;

And *that* every tongue should confess that Jesus Christ *is* Lord, to the glory of God the Father.

Phil. ii. 9-11

A Name above every Name

THIS is the other side of the subject we last considered. Then, we contemplated the descent; now, the ascent: the one, His humiliation; the other, the glory to which God hath exalted Him. We ought to put this passage alongside of Eph. i. 15-23, where the Apostle asserts that God displayed in the person of Jesus His mightiest power, when He raised Him from the dead, and set Him at His own right hand, far above all principality and power, might, and dominion, and every name that is named, not only in this world, but in that which is to come. Indeed all through the New Testament the Father's agency in the exaltation of His Son is distinctly accentuated; and we are constantly reminded of the contrast between the action of men, who with wicked hands crucified and slew Him, and the action of God, who raised Him from the dead.

There are two interpretations, which are suggested by the Authorised and Revised Versions. We are told in the R.V. that God highly exalted Him, and gave Him *the* name which is above every name—the emphasis on the definite *the;* and if we should accept this rendering, it would convey the meaning that the infinite God gave to Jesus, His perfected Servant, His own incommunicable name of Jehovah. The name which is above every name is manifestly the name of Jehovah, which the Jews held to be so sacred that they never mentioned it, never even wrote it. It is important for us to realise that in Jesus Christ there blend at this moment the perfected beauty of the Man and the excelling glory of Jehovah—the glory which He had with the Father before the world was made. That is so deep and blessed a truth that we may be quite prepared to admit it is included in the meaning here, for our Saviour is God. **Phil. ii. 9-11**

But after looking carefully into the matter from every point of view, it seems better to come back to the conclusion suggested by the Authorised Version—that the name of Jesus, which was given to Him in His birth, has been recognised as the highest type of being in the whole universe, and that this name, or more especially the nature for which the name stands, is the loftiest and supreme type of character, which is highly exalted above all other characters and types of being. His is the conquering name; the name which shall become victorious; the name which is destined to supremacy—the name of Jesus. It was given to Him first by the angel Gabriel, when in his annunciation to the mother he said, 'Thou shalt conceive and bring forth a son, and shalt call his name Jesus.' And when Joseph was considering

The Name of Jesus

Phil. ii. 9-11

whether or not he should put away Mary, then espoused to him but not yet married, the angel of God, in a dream, told him to take to himself Mary his wife, because she would bear a son, to whom they must give the name Jesus. This name of Jesus was borne by our Lord throughout His earthly life, and often used by His apostles after His ascension, as the spell and talisman of victory, when they wrought miracles in His name. It is repeatedly referred to in the Epistles, and especially in that to the Hebrews, and evidently stands for the highest type of being. In the whole realm of existence this is the name which is above every name, that at the name of Jesus, the Saviour, every knee should bow in heaven, in earth, and in hades.

Here is Instruction

(1) We obtain instruction. We are familiar with the phrase, 'Survival of the fittest;' by which we understand that amid the shocks and collisions of creation certain types of creature-life, stronger than others, broad-shouldered and powerful, have pushed their way to the front, and have crushed out the weaker. Amid the strife chronicled by history, certain races of mankind inevitably go down, whilst others forge their way to the front and hold positions of supremacy. Similarly, in the life of the world around us, where everything is being searched and tested to the uttermost by the ordeal of time, probation, and trial, certain types of character are constantly being thrust downward, or hurled against the wall in the impetuous rush, whilst others come easily to the front. Thus, perpetually, different types of ideal and character are acknowledged as supreme.

The Name of Names

As we look around us, in the great arena of life, Phil. ii.
we are often disposed to imagine that the type of 9-11
character represented by power, by the giant's grip, by sinew and muscle, is the supreme and victorious one. At other times we are disposed to think that the type of the scientist and philosopher, the man of wise thought and penetrating investigation, is the elect, the ideal type. Again we are disposed to think that the man of wealth, who by his ingenuity has succeeded in accumulating a fortune or in building up a great business, exhibits the ideal type. Thus amid the cross-lights of this world we are greatly perplexed; for when we turn to the life of Jesus Christ, the sweet, gentle, self-denying, and forgiving life, which appeared to be unable to hold its own against the antagonism and malice of men, we are apt to conclude that that type at least is too tender, too gentle, too retiring and unobtrusive to become the dominant type. Yes, we exclaim, the race is to the strong, the sceptre for the wise, the throne for the man of wealth; but the cross is for the character that lives to love and forgive, and save. It is good, therefore, to come into the sanctuary of God, to leave behind us our newspapers and novels, the standards of the market-place and the forum, and to submit our minds beneath the influence of this word which lets in eternity upon time, which allows the light that plays around the throne of God to strike in upon us; and, as we see things for one brief hour, not from the standpoint of our fellows, but of the angels—not judging by the standards of this world, but by those of the other world into which we so soon shall come

Phil. ii. 9-11

—we shall find that the dominant type of character which is to endure, to last supreme when all other types of character, which men have worshipped and idolised, have passed away as the mists of winter before the summer, is the name and nature of Jesus Christ, the Saviour and Redeemer of men.

This is what God hath chosen. Here is the survival of the fittest. Here is the supreme conception of character. This, this is what eternity enthrones. This is what dominates angels and demons. The nature that stoops, loves, forgives, saves; *this* is the ideal type. God hath given Him a name above every name—Jesus, Saviour.

Here is Encouragement

(2) We get great encouragement. It is of infinite importance to know what God loves best. We are destined to live with Him for ever, to see Him face to face, and be for ever in His presence. It is of the highest importance, therefore, to us, to know what is His chosen ideal, that we may begin to shape ourselves by it, that we may emulate it, that we may ourselves seek to be endued by it, so that hereafter we may be taken to the bosom of God as His chosen friends and children. If we desire to know a man we must converse with him, enter his study, handle and look at his books, and gaze round the walls at the pictures he has chosen to adorn them.

If we know a man's ideal, we know him. If we can only get God's ideal, we may know Him. Where can we find it? In creation?—No, not His deepest. In proverb and prophecy?—No, not His deepest. In angels excelling in strength?—No, not

His deepest. In the perfection of moral character? That is nearer, but it is not His deepest. The name that is dearest to God is *Jesus*; and the character which is dearest to God is that which bears, forgives, and loves even to death, that it may save. That which God sets His heart upon for evermore is redemptive love, which He glorifies, raising it to the highest place that heaven affords. Phil. ii. 9-11

'Ah, we will not fear Thee more, our God! We have stood under the thunder-peal hurtling through the air, and trembled; we have beheld the lightning-flash revealing our sin and making us cry for shelter; we have watched Thy march through history, and there have been traces of blood and tears behind on Thy track; and as we look out into the eternal future our hearts stand still. We are but leaves in the great forest of existence; bursting bubbles upon the mighty ocean of being; but when we come to see that Thine ideal is in the Divine Man who died for us, we fear Thee no more, but approach with the confidence of a little child; for if Thou dost love the Man Christ Jesus, and we love Him too, we can meet Thee in the Cross with its dying agony.' It is a great encouragement to know that God's ideal is the Man who died.

Our God seems sometimes to come near us and say: 'There is never a soul that stoops, stripping itself that it may wash the feet of another; there is never a soul that sheds tears over the ruin of those it loves, as Jesus did on the Mount of Olives over Jerusalem; there is never a soul that pours out its life-blood even unto death; there is never a soul

Phil. ii. 9-11

that denies itself to the uttermost, that is not dear to Me. I notice it, though the great world passes by unwitting and careless; I bend over those who tread in the earthly pathway trodden by My Son, My well beloved; and though the midnight darkness may gather over the head, extorting the cry, "My God, my God, why hast Thou forsaken?" I do not forget, I cannot forsake; and presently, when the earth has passed away like the shadow of the cloud upon the hills, I will gather such, and bear them upward, taking them to My bosom, and enthroning them right and left of My Son. He that drinks the cup which Jesus drank of, and is baptised with the baptism with which he was baptised, though forgotten, ignored, crushed and trampled underfoot by men, shall sit beside the Son of Man in His kingdom.'

Oh, let us take heart, as we think of God's ideal; let us be encouraged, for now we know what God is, and that ultimately He will vindicate our work of faith, and labour of love, and patience of hope.

Here is Exhortation

(3) We get exhortation. The name of Jesus is, then, dear to God. What then? Let it be your plea, for it is said that whosoever believeth in that Name shall receive remission of sins. Convicted sinner, longing to have a clue to the maze, go at this moment into the presence of the great God and plead the name of Jesus. Let your one cry be founded upon what He was, and is; and just so soon as you utter that name, in the spirit of the name, God accepts, forgives, and saves.

The Name of Names

Live in that name—in the temper and character of Jesus—day by day; let His Gospel imbue and colour your character; let the imitation of the life of Jesus be the one object of your ambition. There is no other clue to life amid the misery and sorrow of the world. Sometimes it seems hard to remember that children laugh, that the sun shines yet, that the crocuses and snowdrops are preparing to break through the clods of winter. We live oppressed beneath the infinite anguish and agony of the world; it is so dark, so terrible with its sin and sorrow, with its overcrowding and drink and passion; and there is one's own broken life, and all the mystery and perplexity of God's dealings. We can find no clue to it except to follow the ideal of Christ, living to save; every day by patient and tender forbearance making someone happier; lifting the burden from some shoulder, sending a rift of light into some darkened heart. There is no other clue for the difficulty and perplexity of life.

Phil. ii. 9-11

Follow Christ

Sunday School teacher, never let the lesson pass without allowing the Name of Jesus Christ to mingle with your words, like the breath of flowers in the summer air. Preacher, see to it that that Name rings through your utterances, your first word and your last. It is the only spell and talisman of victory; it is the one name that will overcome the power of the devil in temptation, and before which the evil spirits that beset us in our hours of weakness and depression give back. It is the watchword for those who approach the portals of eternity; the talisman of victory in the hour of death.

Speak of Christ

Phil. ii. 9-11 As soon as you utter the name of Jesus, you arrest the Divine ear. Therefore in every prayer, before you break out into adoration, praise, confession, or entreaty, speak in the ear of God that name. Remember that Jesus said: Whatsoever ye ask the Father in My Name, in My Nature, according to the ideal of My life, He will give you. Let the name of Jesus winnow out of your prayers everything proud, selfish, and vindictive; let them be poured like liquid and gleaming metal into that precious mould.

Reverence His Name

Reverence that name. 'In the name of Jesus every knee shall bow.' Let us never utter it without the prefix *Lord.* Let Him be always the *Lord* Jesus. If God speaks His name with marked emphasis, we must treat it with devout reverence. I greatly shrink from too great familiarity with the precious name of our Lord. A man has to be very near the Great Brother who can call him familiarly by His name.

Confess Him

'And every tongue confess.' Let us confess that He is Lord. God the Father has made Him His ideal type; make Him your ideal type. God has just put the sceptre into His hand, do you put the sceptre into His hand also. God has enthroned Him, do you enthrone Him too, and to-day look up and say: 'Henceforth, Blessed Jesus, Thou shalt be Lord and King; Lord of my life, King of my mind and heart; my Lord and my God.'

And remember that that is the one hope of the future. That name of Jesus, whispered first by Gabriel to Mary and to Joseph, spread through a

comparatively small circle of His immediate followers, Phil. ii. 9-11
but at Pentecost the Holy Ghost caught it up, and spoke it in thunder; and ever since it has been spreading through the world and through the universe, and we are yet to see the time when the loftiest angels shall bow beneath it, when all men shall own it, and the very demons acknowledge it. 'Jesus I know, and Paul I know,' was the sad confession of a fallen spirit centuries ago.

This name of our Lord—the last name spoken on earth, the first name uttered in heaven—the name that comprehends grace, the name that spells glory, for He has gone to prepare a place for us. We have passed the shortest day; yonder is the spring and summer of the morning land, and we anticipate the time when we shall sit with Him; bearing that name with Him; and perhaps going forth to all parts of the universe to tell of it, to kindle hearts and lives with it, to unfold, as only redeemed men can, the full meaning and significance of the name Jesus.

11

THE DIVINE ENERGY IN THE HEART

Philippians 2:12,13

WHEREFORE, my beloved, as ye have always obeyed, not as in my presence only, but now much more in my absence, work out your own salvation with fear and trembling.

For it is God which worketh in you both to will and to do of *His* good pleasure.

Phil. ii. 12, 13

THIS text stands between two remarkable injunctions, the first personal — 'Work out your own salvation with fear and trembling'; the second relative—'Do all things without murmurings and disputings; that ye may be blameless and harmless, children of God without rebuke.'

A Personal Injunction

The personal injunction—'Work out your own salvation.' There is a sense in which we are saved *from guilt and the wrath of God* directly we come to the Cross; but there is a sense also in which our salvation *from the power of sin* will not be complete until we stand before God in perfect beauty, and in that sense we have to work it out. God gives us salvation in the germ, but the growth of the tree of our life has to elaborate this primal thought. And we are to do it with 'fear and trembling,' because so much is involved for ourselves and for others, for evermore, if the work is left incomplete. This is the great aim to which all other aims must be subservient —the accomplishment of our soul's salvation, God and we working together. As the husbandman and God work together for the harvest, and as the miner and God work together for the provision of coal in our homes and factories, so we are to work together with God for the full accomplishment of His purpose and our blessedness, in the ultimate salvation of our souls from every evil ingredient. This is a very deep, searching, and important work. Are you engaged in it? Phil. ii. 12, 13

A Relative Injunction

The relative injunction—your attitude to others. 'That ye may be *harmless*,' *i.e.* that your life shall not injure another ; *blameless*, *i.e.* that no one should have any proper blame to attach to you ; *without rebuke*, *i.e.* in the sight of God. And this, not in heaven, but in the midst of 'a crooked and perverse generation.' A traveller in Japan was surprised to find a country given up to arctic winter, in which, nevertheless, there is the abundant tropical growth of oranges and bamboos. He was surprised, whilst the winds were sweeping across the snowy, icy plains of Japan, to find all these tropical plants, which he could only account for by the fact that the country had been volcanic, and that the hidden fire still burnt under the soil, so that, whilst winter reigns in the climate, summer reigns in the heart of the earth, and therefore the tropical plants are able to thrive. And we, in the midst of a very frigid, arctic world, a rebellious generation, are called to live the tropical life of eternity, to be blameless, harmless, and without rebuke. A man may say to himself, It is impossible for me to realise those two injunc-

Phil. ii. 12, 13

tions; but our text lies between them and says, Do not despair, do not abandon hope of being harmless, blameless, and without rebuke, for God will assume the responsibility of making you obedient to His own ideal—'It is God which worketh in you both to will and to work, for His good pleasure.' Work out what He works in.

Six Dominant Notes

Now this sublime text strikes six dominant notes: God's Personality—'it is God'; God's Immanence—'in you'; God's Energy—'worketh in you'; God's Morality—He works in you 'to will'; God's Efficiency—He works in you 'to work'; God's ultimate Satisfaction—'for His own good pleasure.'

* * *

God's Personality

GOD'S PERSONALITY.—'It is God that—' Take away *it*, and transpose the other words—*God is.* Or if you like to strike out the word *is*, you leave the one great word *God.* And God is the answer to every question of the mind, to every trembling perturbation of the heart, to every weakness of appetite, and to every strong hurricane of temptation. The soul, the lonely individual soul, not knowing whence it has come, knowing almost as little whither it goes, confronting the question of weakness and sin and death and eternity, and the deep, deep problem of moral evil, can only answer every complaint by the one all-sufficient, all-comprehending monosyllable *God.* This is our one sheet-anchor—God made us, God knew our constitution, God knew our environment, God knew our temptation, the temptations that would assail us, and yet God redeemed us to Himself, and made us His own by the blood of Christ.

Now, if He be a Being of perfect benevolence, He cannot have done so much without assuming to Himself the responsibility of realising the object of the tears, longings, and prayers, which He has put by His own hand within our nature; and, therefore, we must throw back on Him the responsibility (we doing our part), of making us blameless, harmless, and unrebukable before Him. **Phil. ii. 12, 13**

* * *

God's Immanence

God's Immanence.—Distinguish between justification and sanctification. In justification, which is an instantaneous act upon the part of God, as soon as the soul of man trusts Christ, God imputes to man the righteousness of Jesus Christ, so that he stands before God, in Christ, accepted and beloved. But if that were all it would resemble those curious Eastern processions where they marshal all the beggars of the market-place, and fling over their shoulders white or purple dresses embroidered with gold, so that the procession is composed of a number of the raggedest, dirtiest, laziest men in the kingdom, who look for an hour respectable. And if justification were all, God would simply throw white robes upon us. But our hearts would fester; and, therefore, having justified us by an instantaneous act of His grace, He undertakes our sanctification by His immanence (from the Latin word *in* and *maneo* to remain).

Deeper than the body, deeper than the soul with intellect, imagination, and volition, lies the spirit, and into the spirit of man the Spirit of God comes, bringing the germ of the nature of the risen Christ, so that the Holy Spirit reproduces it within us.

Phil. ii. 12, 13

This is the immanence of God; and this is the distinctive peculiarity of our holy religion—that God can be in us, not robbing us of individuality, but side by side with it, clothing Himself with it, so that just as He was in Isaiah, but Isaiah greatly differs from Jeremiah, just as He was in John, but John was an altogether different man from Peter, so God enters the human spirit, and, without robbing us of our power of volition, individuality, or personality, He waits within, longing to burst through every restraint, and to reveal Himself through us in all the beauty and glory of His nature. Hide yourself, and let God work through you His own perfect ideal.

* * *

God's Energy

God's Energy.—He works. He is not an absentee in creation; He is not an absentee in providence; He is not an absentee in the spirit of man; but He works so unobtrusively that we do not always realise the mighty forces which are at work within us. Froude and Carlyle, in Carlyle's house, had a conversation one day about God's work, and Froude said that God's work in history was like His work in nature, modest, quiet, and unobtrusive. Carlyle replied sadly and solemnly—for it was a day of one of his darker moods—"Ah, but, Froude, God seems to do so little!"—as though he expected that God would resemble a world-conqueror, whose personality is always attracting attention.

If you had been present during creation, as Milton puts it, you might only have heard flute-like music. You would not have heard the voice that said, Light be! or that bade the waters give place. You would not have seen the mighty hands moulding the earth. All would have been done by natural processes, so simply, so ordinarily, you would hardly have recognised the greatness of the Creator. Phil. ii. 12, 13

And so in our heart. O son of man, thou hast not realised it, that all through these years the infinite God has been imprisoned in thy spirit; and thy tears, thy sighs, thy regrets, thy yearnings, the rejuvenation of thy conscience, which thou hast so often affronted and injured,—prove that the Holy, mighty, and loving God is within thy spirit, fretting against the evil as John Howard fretted against the evils of the lazaretto and the prison, longing to make thy heart pure and sweet, if only thou wilt yield to Him.

* * *

The Divine Morality

THE DIVINE MORALITY.—He works in us *to will.* That is, He does not treat us like a machine, He deals with us as moral agents who can say yes and no. He is not going to compel us to be saints, He is not going to force us to be holy. If thou wilt, He much more wills, and thou dost will because He willed before. The will of God wants to take thee up into itself, as the wind that breathes over a city waits to catch up the smoke from a thousand chimney-pots, and waft it on its bosom through the heavens.

You may always know when God is *willing* within you—first, by a holy discontent with yourself. You are dissatisfied with all that you have ever done, and been. Secondly, you aspire; you see above you the snow-capped peaks, and your heart longs to climb and to stand there. Thirdly, these are followed by the appreciation of the possibility of your being

Phil. ii. 12, 13

blameless and harmless and without rebuke. If a man refuses to believe that he can be a saint, he never will become one. If a man says, I cannot hope to be more than conqueror, God Himself cannot save him. When the Spirit of God is within you, there rises up a consciousness that you have the capacity for the highest possible attainments, because you were made and redeemed in the image of God, and because the germ of the Christ-nature has been sown in your spirit. Two men go through a picture-gallery. Each sees the same masterpiece. One says, I cannot imagine how that can be done. The other man says, I also am a painter. That second man is capable of producing a picture which also shall outlive. You must believe that you can be a saint, even you. You must dare to believe it, because the Christ-germ is sown in your character, and because God is working in you to will and to do. Fourthly, the determination, I will. There should be a moment in the history of us all when each shall say—Cost what it may, I will not yield again; I will arise to be what God wants to make me; I will yield myself to Him; I will reckon myself to be dead indeed unto sin, and alive unto God through Jesus Christ; I will yield myself to the power that worketh in me. Discontent, aspiration, appreciation of the possibilities of saintliness, and resolve.

The will of God is working in you to-day. Cannot you take those four steps? Are you going back to live the old self-indulgent life? If so, these words will be a curse to you, for nothing injures the soul so much as to know the truth and yet fall back into the ditch.

* * * Phil. ii. 12, 13

God's Work for Work

'He Works to Work.'—Does God allow babes to want milk, and then, in the eternal ordering of things, not provide milk? Does not the longing of the little child argue that somewhere, presumably in the mother's breast, there is the supply? Do the swallows begin to gather around the eaves of our houses, longing for a sunny clime, and is there no such realm of sunshine to be reached over land and sea? Do the young lions in the winter roar for food, that God does not furnish? Do you think that God is going to give us this discontent with ourselves, this yearning after Himself, and is going to mock us? That would be the work of a devil. If you hold that God is good and loving and holy, your very aspirations are a proof that He who works in you to *will*, is prepared to work in you to *do*. But, till now, we have done so much by our own resolutions, that we have shut His doing out. If only we would relinquish our efforts after sanctification, as once we relinquished those after justification, and if we said to Him: 'Great God, work out Thine own ideal in my poor weak nature,' He would will and He would work. God's morality and God's efficiency are co-equal.

* * *

God's Satisfaction

God's Satisfaction.—'For His good pleasure.' When He made the world, He said it was very good; then sin came, and selfishness; and the dull dark ages passed, till Jesus came, who opened His nature to the Father, though He were the Son of God. The mystery of the Incarnation lies in this:

Phil. ii. 12, 13

our Lord gave up the exercise of His inherent deity as the Son of God, and became dependent on the Father, and the Father wrought perfectly through the yielded nature of the Son. Oh, ponder this! The Father wrought perfectly in the yielded nature of Jesus, and the result was summed up in the cry, 'This is my beloved Son, in whom I am well pleased.' In some such manner it is possible to walk worthy of God unto all pleasing. It is possible to have this testimony, even in our mortal life, that we have pleased God. At the end of every day, as we lie down to sleep—we may hear the whisper of God's voice saying, 'Dear child, I am pleased with you.' But you can only have it by allowing Him in silence, in solitude, in obedience, to work in you, to will and to do of His own good pleasure.

An Appeal to you

Will you begin now? He may be working in you to confess to that fellow-Christian that you were unkind in your speech or act. Work it out. He may be working in you to give up that line of business about which you have been doubtful lately. Give it up. He may be working in you to be sweeter in your home, and gentler in your speech. Begin. He may be working in you to alter your relations with some with whom you have dealings that are not as they should be. Alter them. This very day let God begin to speak, and work and will; and then work out what He works in. God will not work apart from you, but He wants to work through you. Let Him. Yield to Him, and let this be the day when you shall begin to live in the power of the mighty Indwelling One.

12

STARS TO SHINE: VOICES TO SPEAK

Philippians 2:14-16

Do all things without murmurings and disputings:
That ye may be blameless and harmless, the sons of God, without rebuke, in the midst of a crooked and perverse nation, among whom ye shine as lights in the world:
Holding forth the word of life; that I may rejoice in the day of Christ, that I have not run in vain, neither laboured in vain.

Phil. ii. 14-16

Retrospect

WHENEVER we review the past, our souls are filled with gratitude to God for all the wonderful way that He has led us; but, as we thank Him, we are filled with a sorrowful and infinite regret, and we cannot forget, amid the many mercies we recall, the story of our repeated failure and shortcoming. Yet, mingling with gratitude and sorrow are hope, resolve, and the decision that the past shall be buried by the past, and that we will step forward to an entirely new life of prayer, consecration, and devotion. These three words—thankfulness, confession, and resolve—surely characterise the feelings of all intelligent and thoughtful persons, who by regeneration, through the Holy Spirit applying the Word of Truth, and by adoption into the family of God, have been dissociated from this sinful and adulterous generation, and are

Phil. ii. 14-16

reckoned among the children of the resurrection, heirs of God and joint heirs with Christ.

In this paragraph we are brought face to face with the Divine ideal—an ideal which, alas! we have too little realised, but which henceforth shall be realised with new hope. We discover, also, the infinite sources of power which we have not always realised—that God works in us. We are also taught to set ourselves, with new persistency, to the working out of that which God is working in.

* * *

Our Ideal as the Children of God

The Negative Side

If you will follow out the paragraph step by step, link by link, you will see that there is the negative and the positive side. There is, *first*, the NEGATIVE SIDE. 'Do all things without murmurings and disputings, that ye may be the sons of God, without rebuke,' or, as the R.V. puts it, more accurately, *without blemish.* To be without blemish is perpetually held up as the supreme ideal of the Christian life. 'He chose us in Him before the foundation of the world, that we should be holy and without blemish before Him in love.' 'That it (the Church) should be holy and without blemish.' 'To present you holy and without blemish.' The Lamb of God was without blemish, and we are called to be the same. There is the more necessity that we should rise to the level of our high calling, because our lives are cast into the midst of a community of distorted vision and oblique ways—'a crooked and perverse generation.' This description of society is as true to-day as it ever was. Whether we look at political or social life, the newspapers or the streets, the tone of conversation in the drawing-rooms or on ocean steamers, everything vindicates the adjectives of the Apostle. Phil. ii. 14-16

The prime method of being without blemish is to do all things 'without murmurings and disputings.' Do not allow yourselves to fall into discontented moods, and do not indulge in bitter conflict with others. *Murmurings* stand for all sorts of ill-concealed, half-checked, and half-uttered complaints. They are the low grumblings of a man who is swayed inwardly by impatient thoughts and hard feelings. *Disputings* are murmurings come to the surface, and breaking out into captious and angry discussions. Keep the heart and the tongue right by the grace of God, and you will be blameless and harmless, the sons of God, without blemish.

Blamelessness is faultlessness, stainlessness—correctness in all the externals of life, as Zacharias and Elisabeth were, who walked in all the commandments and ordinances of the Lord *blameless*. *Harmlessness* refers to the essential purity, simplicity, and sincerity, which should characterise all followers of Christ, because there is no admixture of evil thoughts or desires in their aims or conduct.

Our Ideal: The Positive Side

Secondly, there is the POSITIVE side. Phillips Brooks says: 'It is the sincere and deep conviction of my soul, that if the Christian faith does not culminate and complete itself in the effort to make itself known to all the world, that faith appears to me to be a thoroughly unreal and insignificant thing, destitute of power for a single life, and incapable of being convincingly proved to be true.' He says also:

Phil. ii. 14-16

'Always the enlargement of the faith brings the endearment of the faith; and to give the Saviour to others makes Him more thoroughly our own.'

Shine as Stars

Such thoughts were in the Apostle's heart when he urged his converts to *shine and hold forth the word of Life.* (1) If they were Christians at all, they must be *stars* shining amid the darkness of the world. The image before his mind was that of a new star floating into sight, taking its place among the constellations of the skies, and shedding forth its beams, so as to reproduce its own luminosity as widely as possible, though with the stillness which has no audible voice or language. Here is the consistency and beauty of a holy soul, endeavouring to pass on its nature to other souls, that they too may be light in the Lord.

As we look out on nature, we find that the object for which every flower spreads its colour and perfume is to attract the bee, so that it may propagate its kind. The flower must reproduce itself, or show itself unworthy of the Gardener who produced it not for itself alone. Every living thing exists to pass on its nature; and surely the Christian soul cannot be content unless it has sent itself forward into other lives and coming generations.

One of the most interesting studies is that of inductive electricity. When two wires lie side by side, and a stream of electricity is sent through the one, a faint vibration and reproduction of it will be perceived in the other. It is in this way that, on the long lines of American travel, you are able to telegraph from your moving train to the city you are nearing. The wires along the track are sympathetic with the transmitter on the train. For the same reason, when speaking through the telephone, one can hear the murmur of other wires. It is not that they really touch, but they are deeply sympathetic. Phil. ii. 14-16

Our Influence on other Souls

There is something like this in our influence upon other souls. There are induced currents for good or bad. You, as a child of God, cannot come in contact with other men who belong to this crooked and perverse generation, without starting within them the vibrations of your own holiness, the yearning for something better than they are, the appetite, the hunger and thirst, after the unseen and the eternal, the condemnation of their sin, and the creation within them of the vibrations and waves of desire to be other than they are. It is also true that you cannot come in contact with a bad man, whose mind is steeped in vice, and whose life is full of base and disgraceful actions, without a corresponding current being induced in yourself. We are always, for good or bad, affecting those who are in close contact with us, and this altogether apart from our volition, and simply by the strength of our character.

Hence it is that Richter, the great German thinker, says: 'If thou knowest how every black thought of thine, and every jealous thought, takes root outside of thee, and goes on for half a century pushing and boring its healing or poisonous roots through the earth, ah, how carefully wouldst thou grow, how carefully wouldst thou choose and think!' And Bishop Huntingdon is on the same line when he says: 'There is some nameless influence going

Phil. ii. 14-16

out from the very least conscious thing in God's creation, which alters and shapes in its measure every man, woman, and child within its influence.'

A great Responsibility

It is almost terrible to live with these thoughts pressing on one's heart—that one can never speak a word, never transact a piece of business, that one's face is never seen lighted up with the radiance of God, or clouded and despondent, without it being made harder or easier for other men to live a good life. Every one of us, every day, resembles Jeroboam, the son of Nebat, who made other men sin; or we are lifting other men into the light, and peace, and joy of God. No man liveth to himself, and no man dieth to himself; but the life of every one is telling upon an increasing number of mankind. What a solemn responsibility it is to live! What infinite regret should oppress our souls at the thought that we have flung shadows over so many lives which God meant to be happy; that we have put so many stumbling-blocks in people's ways to whom God meant that we should offer stepping-stones; that our life has been for the shame and sorrow rather than for the uplifting and comfort of those around us!

Ours can never be sunshine, the intrinsic light of the sun. At the most we shall never be able to diffuse more than the borrowed light of the star; but this is something, and we may shine amid the dark night which has rested on mankind ever since the sun went down on Calvary in blood-red skies. Ere long the dawn will break on the sky, and we shall become invisible amid the radiance of the coming Lord.

(2) Besides being a star, we must be a voice; *we are to hold forth the word of Life.* We cannot hold forth the word without words. It is our duty to speak to those in our immediate circle, that there may be no regret at the end of life. This wonderful gift of human speech, the most marvellous faculty with which any one of us is endowed, must be used to pass on the word of the Kingdom. Lay yourself before God, and your mouth in the very dust, and ask that the Holy Spirit may take your lips, and set them on fire for Himself, that you may be able not only to *shine* with the mild radiance of a stainless and beautiful character, but that you may *utter* the word of Life to those who have never given heed to it. Surely the contemplation of such an ideal must fill us with infinite regret. As we go over item after item, we see that there is not one trait to which we can lay claim without considerable misgiving. We are not without blemish! We have not refrained from murmurings and disputings! We have not been blameless and harmless! As we catch sight of God's ideal, we abhor ourselves. As we hear the perfect music, we lament our own discordant notes. As we see the solemn troops and sweet societies of Heaven, we realise how coarse and unrefined our manners are. There cannot be an evening in our life in which, as we review the day, we do not require the precious Blood of Christ.

Phil. ii. 14-16

Voices to speak for God

*　　*　　*

The past is gone, never to be recalled; and if we are to trust our resolutions, we must certainly and inevitably fall again. But our text says that God is

The Power by which the Ideal is rendered possible

Phil. ii. 14-16 in us; that God, who makes the universe His home, has come to dwell in our hearts, not as a stranger who tarries for a night, but as an abiding, indwelling guest; and that our God is in us to will and to work of His own good pleasure. We have often been conscious of it. Have there not often been within us induced currents of Divine electricity, promptings and inspirations to unselfishness, purity, and devotion, which, alas! we have too often resisted? Ponder again the wondrous message!

God works in us to will. He does not overpower our will, or treat us as automata which He can move at His choice. He approaches us as intelligent beings, who may refuse, as they may accept and yield. At the most He can only suggest certain lines of conduct, but it is left to us to say whether we will make them our own or not. Do you not sometimes feel rising up within you a great desire, a yearning, a drawing, a purpose to be other than you are? Ah! this is God working in you to wish and will. Be very thankful, because you know that God is taking pains with your character, only be sure to let Him have your eager and complete response.

God works in us to work. God never works in us to will without empowering us to perform that to which He prompts. He has with Him a sufficiency of power equivalent to our necessity, and if we will turn to Him for it, He will enable us to carry out every prompting of His will. We may not remember the moment when He entered; we may not have heard the sound of His feet along the passage-way of our heart; He may have stolen in on the morning light, in the waft of the wind, or on the fragrance of flowers—but He is in thy soul and mine. He is come to take our side against sin. The Father waits to make the child like Himself, first by prompting him to will good things, and then by energising him to do the things He wills. That is our hope; and our only hope for the coming days, that they may be better than the past, is the recognition that our ideal is God's for us, and He waits to make it a living fact. Phil. ii. 14-16

* * *

Our Duty to work out what He works in

Is there anything in life or heart which has of late caused you solicitude? Have you been doubtful about a certain line of conduct? Has something which you did in the past arisen and made you feel that you ought to make restitution and reparation? Is there some one habit, a method of life, an inner idol, an unopened cupboard, which has not been consecrated absolutely to Him? Do you realise that there is the constant pressure by Another than yourself dealing with it? Do you hear the thud of the engine deep down in your soul; the movement of the piston that sends the quiver of the vibration through the whole of your being? Be very thankful, for God is come to fight the evil of your nature, as a mother sets herself beside her child to fight the disease which is sapping his life.

But God's efforts on our behalf will be abortive unless we work out what He works in. If He wills in us to break with some evil habit, we must will the same. Our will must yield to His, as the skiff to the stream that bears it on its current. If He bids us

Phil. ii. 14-16

take up our bed and walk, we must dare to believe that we can do it, and availing ourselves of His might, we must spring to our feet. If He sends us on His divine errands, we must not be rebellious nor hold ourselves back. Our salvation lies in achieving deliverance from every form of sin, and it is only by degrees that we learn all that sin is, and become emancipated from its dominion and love.

With Fear and Trembling

Let us do this 'with fear and trembling.' If an illustrious artist spends a morning with one of his students, helping him to finish some picture at which he has been working hard but unsuccessfully, the young man does not fear the artist, but trembles lest he may not make the best possible use of his kindness. So, my soul, when the great God comes to thee, and says, 'I am going to save thee from thy sins,' thou must take good heed to garner up all His gracious help with miserly care, full of anxiety lest thou shouldest fail to avail thyself of the least trust, the smallest prompting. He will do His work effectually and thoroughly; let Him have full scope, and thou shalt be more than satisfied.

Oh, Thou who workest through the universe, who fulfillest Thine own high purpose, so that seraphs, angels, and all holy beings are infilled by Thee, come to-day and fill us, infill our whole nature, then spirit, soul, and body shall be impenetrated by Thine energy, and shall realise Thine ideal!

13

THE SACRIFICIAL SIDE OF THE CHRISTIAN LIFE

Philippians 2:17,18

YEA, and if I be offered upon the sacrifice and service of your faith, I joy, and rejoice with you all.

For the same cause also do ye joy, and rejoice with me.

AGAIN the Apostle refers to the 'day of Christ.' He was constantly anticipating the coming of the Lord. His early Epistles specially abound in references to that event which would bring to light the hidden things of darkness, and make manifest the counsels of all hearts, so that each man should have his praise from God. He spoke of his being alive and remaining unto the coming of the Saviour, and as anticipating that his mortality would be swallowed up of life. Often, amid his imprisonment, he must have listened for the sounding of the trumpet of God, and the songs which accompanied his returning Lord. Invariably he so lived and laboured, that whenever that day came, whether to close his earthly life or afterwards, he might receive the reward, which would be to him what the crown of amaranth was to the successful competitor in the games.

Phil. ii. 17, 18

* * *

Paul's great Fear

Paul's incessant fear was that he might run or labour in vain. There are many expressions of it. In one place he expresses the fear lest all the work

Phil. ii. 17, 18

which he had built upon the foundation, which God had previously laid, should be burned up, and he should suffer loss; in another he gives utterance to the dread lest he should be a castaway (or rejected) as one who had no right to the prize; here, he uses the words 'in vain' as though some mistake on his part should obliterate all the results of the work, which he had laboriously sought to achieve for his Lord.

How is it with us?

A very solemn inquiry is suggested to us all. Are we running in vain? Are we labouring in vain? Life is full of running to and fro, and incessant labour, but we may gravely ask whether at the end there will be aught to show commensurate with the energy we have expended. So many days are lived in vain! So many books are written in vain! So many sermons preached in vain! So many philanthropic activities expended in vain!

A Condition of Success

It is, however, certain that before any service that we do for God or man is likely to be of lasting and permanent benefit, it must be saturated with our heart's blood. That which costs us nothing will not benefit others. If there is no expenditure of tears and prayer, if that love, of which the Apostle speaks in another place, which costs, is wanting, we may speak with the tongues of men and of angels, may know all mysteries and all knowledge, may bestow all our goods to feed the poor, but it will profit nothing. Let us rather seek to be poured forth as a libation than to do much without feeling the least travail of soul. As the fertility of Egypt in any year is in direct proportion to the height that the waters of the Nile measure on the Nilometer, so the amount of our real fruitfulness in the world is gauged by the expenditure of our spiritual force. Phil. ii. 17, 18

It was because Moses was prepared to be blotted from the Book of God for his people that he carried them for forty years through the desert, and deposited them on the very borders of the Promised Land. It was because Jesus wept over Jerusalem that He was able to send a Pentecost on the guilty city. It was because Paul was prepared to be accursed for his brethren according to the flesh, that he was able to turn so many from darkness to light, and from the power of Satan unto God. It is when Zion travails that she brings forth her children. No heart pangs, no spiritual seed.

The Call for Sacrifice

The Christian life should be a sacrifice. Where faith in Christ is a reality, it will lead not simply to a life service, which becomes a *liturgy,* but also to *sacrifice.* 'I beseech you, therefore, brethren, by the mercies of God to present your bodies a living sacrifice, holy, well-pleasing to God, which is your reasonable service.'

There is only one sacrifice which can take away sin, and which was offered once for all. 'When He had offered one sacrifice for sins, forever He sat down on the right hand of God': 'By one offering He hath perfected forever them that are sanctified.' But the whole Church of God is called to follow the Master's steps in the sacrifice of her life for men. She must fill up that which is behind of the sufferings of Christ; she must be prepared to suffer with Him; she must surrender the joy that is set before her of ease, and

Phil. ii. 17, 18

luxury, and earthly power, in order that she may go out to her Lord without the camp, bearing His reproach. He is the Lamb of God which taketh away the sin of the world, and by His one sufficient sacrifice has opened the way into peace, but there is a sacrifice of what the world deems choicest and best in order that the highest interest of men should be better served, which is the peculiar prerogative, not only of the Church of Christ collectively, but of each individual soul.

Have we our Sacrifice?

Is there sacrifice in your life and mine? I knew, for instance, of the case of a young girl, who promised her mother upon her dying bed, that she would not accept an offer of marriage until she had seen the younger children well started in life, and had performed the last offices for her father. I do not here comment upon the unwisdom of a mother exacting such a pledge from her child, but only cite the fact. As a result, when, three years after her mother's death, Love looked into the window of that girl's soul, and one who was altogether suitable for her asked her to be his wife, she felt bound to refuse, and nobly stood by her charge until the whole family passed out of her care into homes of their own. It was a supreme relinquishment of all that a woman holds dearest, but how noble it was!

Is not sacrifice of this sort constantly being demanded of us, have we not all to turn from the doors that stand wide open on our mountains of transfiguration, in order to descend into the valley, where the cross of self-denial stands with wide-open arms, awaiting us? Whenever such is the case, our faith is working out in sacrifice, our obedience to the will of God is enabling us to surrender all things, that we may more efficiently do the high work of Jesus for others. We may well doubt whether we are true followers of the Crucified, or have entered into any true experience of His religion, unless there is the trace of the Cross somewhere, whether known to men, or known only to Christ. **Phil. ii. 17, 18**

When a deluded man set himself up as the Christ of to-day, the indignant crowd that gathered around the doors of his church demanded that he should show them his hands, meaning that if he were the Christ, the marks of the nails would certainly be apparent. It was a just request. People know well enough that Christ stands for sacrifice, and that His followers can expect no better treatment than He experienced. And again we may put the question to ourselves: Does our faith cost us anything, and is our service to man and God often sealed by blood?

Paul ready to be offered

The Apostle was willing to yield his life's blood as a libation. Moses said, 'He that offereth his oblation must offer wine for the drink offering, the fourth part of an hin shall he prepare with the burnt offering or for the sacrifice, for each lamb' (Numbers xv. 5). This was doubtless in the Apostle's mind when he spoke of being poured out as a drink offering upon the sacrifice and service of their faith. (See R.V. margin.)

What unity there was between his sufferings in Rome and theirs in Philippi! It seemed to him as though they had reached a common altar, and were engaged in one common act of devotion. Not only

Phil. ii. 17, 18

did their faith lead them to considerable sacrifice in order to supply his needs, but it was likely to extort a still greater surrender, even of life itself in the defence of the truth; but in that same cause it was not improbable that sooner or later he would have to shed his blood. There was indeed an *if* in the case. '*If* I am offered,' etc., but whilst Nero was on the throne, and the hatred of the Jews so virulent, there was little hope that he would escape.

The prospect, however, did not fill him with dread. On the contrary, he anticipated it as though it were a marriage. The thought that he was consummating the faith and service of the Philippians, who had first learnt to love God through his ministry, was a cause of infinite delight.

The Joy of Sacrifice

It was thus that the martyrs pressed to the scaffold and stake, rejoicing that they were counted worthy to suffer for Christ's name. So great was the enthusiasm in the early days, that the Church authorities had to publish edicts, prohibiting the Christians of their time from hazarding their lives, or throwing them needlessly away. When once the soul has caught sight of the true significance of life, and has learnt the privilege which is within its reach, of identifying itself with the Son of God in His great act of Redemption, a similar glow of joy begins to cast its radiance over passages of life that hitherto had been dark and forbidding. The joy of the Lord becomes a source of altogether new strength. Partnership with Jesus in the redemption of the world, opens the door to partnership in those fountains of blessedness that rise within His soul, and to which He referred, when He said, 'Your heart shall rejoice, and your joy no one taketh from you': 'These things have I said unto you that My joy might remain in you, and that your joy might be full.' Phil. ii. 17, 18

14

'NOT SORROW UPON SORROW'

Philippians 2:19-30

BUT I trust in the Lord Jesus to send Timotheus shortly unto you, that I also may be of good comfort, when I know your state.

For I have no man likeminded, who will naturally care for your state.

For all seek their own, not the things which are Jesus Christ's.

But ye know the proof of him, that, as a son with the father, he hath served with me in the gospel.

Him therefore I hope to send presently, so soon as I shall see how it will go with me.

But I trust in the Lord that I also myself shall come shortly.

Yet I supposed it necessary to send to you Epaphroditus, my brother, and companion in labour, and fellow-soldier, but your messenger, and he that ministered to my wants.

For he longed after you all, and was full of heaviness, because that ye had heard that he had been sick.

For indeed he was sick nigh unto death: but God had mercy on him; and not on him only, but on me also, lest I should have sorrow upon sorrow.

I sent him therefore the more carefully, that, when ye see him again, ye may rejoice, and that I may be the less sorrowful.

Receive him therefore in the Lord with all gladness; and hold such in reputation:

Because for the work of Christ he was nigh unto death, not regarding his life, to supply your lack of service toward me.

Phil. ii. 19-30 THE Bible is so Divine because it is so human. This chapter began with the sorrows of the Son of God; it ends with the sorrow of His Apostle; and the Holy Spirit does not deem it incongruous to deal first with the wonderful condescension of our blessed Master from the supernal Throne to the Cross of shame, and then to turn back to what was transacting in a human breast, of hope and fear, of sorrow and joy, on the banks of the muddy Tiber. So, beloved, however great God is, and however vast the range and circumference of His interests, there is not one tear that you shed, one sorrow that you feel, that is not of exceeding importance and care to Him. The Great God, who, in the Person of His Son, stooped from the Throne to the Cross, and is now exalted above all conception, yet thinks of His prisoner in the hired house at Rome, and sees to it that the pressure of sorrow shall not be too great for the delicate machinery of his frail heart to sustain. **Phil. ii. 19-30**

THE FACTS AS HERE STATED.—The Philippian Church; the Apostle Paul; Timothy; Epaphroditus; God.

The Church at Philippi

(1) *The Church at Philippi* (vv. 25, 30). For ten years the Christians there had not assisted the Apostle; not that they had forgotten him, but because they had had no opportunity. He was in circumstances where they could not reach him. It might have been supposed that they had forgotten, but such love as theirs never forgets. It may not be able to furnish assistance, but it still burns on the altar of the heart.

Be loyal to your love; whatever else you forget in the world, never forget the claims of friendship. Let love be cherished above all other treasures. Trust each other's love, and when there is no sign or token, still believe that your friend is loyal, and only awaiting the moment when his help may reveal an undying, unaltering affection. The

Phil. ii. 19-30

Philippians were only waiting until the time came, the time when they could help best. Give a man bread when he is hungry, drink when he is thirsty, and clothes when he is naked; watch your moment. Ah, if we would but watch the timely moment, when some spirit is failing, when hope threatens to expire, when heart and soul faint, and would strike in then, how many desperate deeds we should arrest, and how many heart-broken ones we should encourage to face with fresh hope the difficulty and responsibility of life! Be true to your friends; trust your friends; redeem the opportunity.

The Imprisoned Apostle

(2) *The Apostle Paul.* He could preach, but he was a handcuffed prisoner; and in that dreary apartment, from which he looked out wearily upon liberty, he was often lonely. He had sent everybody away whom he could trust, except Timothy and Epaphroditus. But he was extremely anxious about the welfare of his Philippian friends; and he knew that they were equally anxious about him; he gave up, therefore, the one man of all others who was dear to him — Timothy — and sent him to bring word about their state, and that they might be comforted in knowing about his. Because the Philippians were so true in their love to him, he counted no sacrifice too great to show his love to them. The man who lives nearest God is always nearest his fellows, and he who is most sensitive towards God is most sensitive towards man, and will rather go without his dearest and nearest, to show how much he is prepared to do to sympathise with and help others. Be always willing to sacrifice

your Timothies if you may give a ray of comfort to the distant friends at Philippi. Phil. ii. 19-30

The Helper, Timothy

(3) *Timothy.* Timothy loved Paul as a child his father (v. 22, R.V.). He had been delicately reared; his constitution was weak, so much so that the Apostle even advised him to take a little wine for his often infirmities; and perhaps he was too sensitive to stand against strong opposition and dislike. But, with all this, he was a man of rare sweetness of disposition and grace of character. He had great faith in the Lord Jesus, and was staunch and loyal to his friend. Probably his love to Paul strengthened his character, and the demand that Paul made on him brought out his noblest and best, so that young Timothy grew to be a hero under the touch of love. What a wonderful power love is—the right kind of love! There is a selfish, hurtful, harmful love that enervates and injures its objects; there is another, an unselfish love, that draws out the best and noblest, making the timid strong and brave, and eliciting the hero that had lain buried in the soul. Timothy would therefore be sent to Philippi, as soon as the Apostle knew how his trial would turn out; and probably the Apostle would closely follow him (vv. 23, 24).

"My Brother"

(4) *Epaphroditus.* The Apostle speaks of Epaphroditus, who was to carry this Epistle, as the minister and apostle from Philippi, because he had brought the gifts of Philippi over sea and land. He describes him also, with exquisite delicacy, as *My brother.* There is no kinship so close as that brotherhood into which a common love to God

Phil. ii. 19-30

brings two men. 'My brother, my fellow-worker, my fellow-soldier' (v. 25, R.V.). Epaphroditus was a man of much less gift than Paul, yet Paul seemed to forget the disparity and speaks of him as his equal—my fellow-worker and fellow-soldier, because to work for Christ, and to fight side by side in the ranks of Christ's Gospel, must bring soul close to soul.

Epaphroditus, the Suppliant

Epaphroditus is probably referred to as Epaphras in Col. iv. 12, and there we learn that he laboured fervently in prayer, that the distant Churches might be perfect in all the will of God. The word used of this good man's prayer, is *agonise*; he agonised as a gladiator in an amphitheatre, or an athlete in an arena. He was so intense in his intercession for his brethren in the faith, that it seemed as though his very veins stood out as whipcord, and his whole soul was knit into an agony. This simple man prayed so earnestly that Paul said he was like a gladiator wrestling in the amphitheatre. He had fallen sick; perhaps he had taken Roman-fever when diving down into some of the worst parts of Rome to look after lost men, who, like Onesimus, had gone astray, and in one of these terrible dens of infamy, where the air was heavy with disease and impurity, this good man Epaphroditus was taken ill (v. 30). When tidings came to the Apostle, they nearly broke his heart, because he feared that his friend would die, and he be unable to visit him or to help.

Epaphroditus was, however, spared, but in his convalescence was sore troubled, because, somehow, the Philippians had come to hear of his sickness, and would naturally be filled with profound anxiety about it. So delicate is love in its sensitiveness. It is a difficult question to decide how much love ought to tell the loved one. You might have supposed Epaphroditus ought to tell, and would be glad to tell, his Philippian friends. But he thought otherwise. He felt that they had trouble and responsibility and anguish enough, and he did not want to add one additional burden to those who were already weighted to the ground. **Phil. ii. 19-30**

Reticence and Frankness

Perhaps it is wise, when we are so far away from those we love that they cannot possibly help us, to keep back something of the pain and sorrow through which we are going; but with those whom we are meeting day by day we should not be reticent, for reticence is often the death-blow of love. The only thing about which we do well to be reticent to our intimate friends is when we have been slighted or injured. Under such circumstances it is good not to speak, because, maybe, we shall magnify the slight into an actual wrong, whilst if we do not speak about it we shall forget it.

In other things it is well to be frank. Confidence is the native air of love. Those words of Lord Bacon's, in his inimitable essay upon Friendship, are perfectly true. 'We know,' he says, 'that diseases of stoppings and suffocations are most dangerous to the body; and it is not much otherwise in the mind. You may take sarza to open the liver, steel to open the spleen, flower of sulphur for the lungs, castoreum for the brain; but no receipt openeth the heart but a true friend, to whom you may impart griefs, joys, fears, hopes, suspicions,

Phil. ii. 19-30

counsels, and whatever lieth upon the heart to oppress it, in a kind of civil shrift or confession.'

We must admire Epaphroditus, whose love was so sensitive that he said: 'They cannot help me; if they were near enough to nurse me I would tell them, but they are too far away.' But when he knew that tidings of his illness, but not of his convalescence, had reached them, the news almost caused a relapse.

God's Care

(5) *God.* St Paul lived in a very atmosphere of love. Think of it. All around, the world lay in hate, malice, and envy; but in that hired room in Rome there was the intense focus-point of love. In the midst of winter all around, there was summer in that hired house. In the midst of the dark night of heathenism there was the one beautiful spot of heavenly life.

The Philippian gifts were all about the place, showing they had not forgotten him. So far from forgetting them, the Apostle was thinking of sending Timothy, though it seemed like tearing a part of himself away. Timothy was, also, as intent on serving him as a child a father, and daring to share his bonds and shame. In addition, there was Epaphroditus anxious because the Philippians were anxious, and distressed beyond measure because he added to their grief. There was a perfect hothouse of love—palms, fruits, and flowers in a tropical atmosphere amid the wintry climate. And out of all that there came this blessed faith in God that He would not add sorrow to sorrow. Paul said to himself: 'I am quite sure God is just like man, only better. I am quite sure that God is as thoughtful and sensitive as we are about one another. I would not let Epaphroditus die, unless there were some urgent reason to the contrary; if I could spare a servant of mine sorrow I would.' He argued from the love of which he was personally conscious to the love above him, and said: God is like a father, mother, brother, sister, friend, all in one. The most tender, gentle, sensitive being in the whole universe is God, and He will not add sorrow to sorrow. There must be sorrow, that I may learn to sympathise with sorrow, that my heart may be open towards all who suffer; but there will be no needless adding of sorrow to sorrow. What a noble conception is presented to us here of how human love lifts man to understand the Divine love! We argue from the human to the Divine: 'How much more shall your heavenly Father give good things to them that ask Him.' He will not overdrive His flock; nor give us more than we can bear; nor add one drop of needless grief to our heart's burden.

Phil. ii. 19-30

*　　　*　　　*

Christ and Human Friendship

We may Draw Three Conclusions.—First, that *Christ recognises human friendships.* Love is the one thing that makes life worth living. One has said: 'I would rather be condemned to be led out and hung, if I knew one human soul would love me for a week beforehand and honour me afterwards, than live half a century to be nothing to any living creature.' That life is richest which has most true friends; that life is most worth living which is surrounded by the truest and tenderest hearts. But do we prize human love enough? Do we requite it as we should? Are we not too careless of these

Phil. ii. 19-30

pearls of spiritual wealth? Do we not break the necklace and loose the pearls too recklessly? Are there not people in our own home-circle who, if they were to die this week, would haunt our memory with infinite regret? 'George,' she said, 'I was a foolish girl, but I always loved you.' But the kisses that poured from the husband's lips were too late to arrest the death, and undo the lovelessness of his treatment of the one whom he promised to love with all his heart; and he must suffer always afterwards the gnawing of a constant sorrow.

How eminently careful we ought to be to be loyal to love; to be sensitive not needlessly to hurt, and never to fall beneath the high standard put by Jesus Christ in his loyalty to Mary, Martha, and Lazarus, and the rest. Jesus Christ recognises human love. Lacordaire, the great French preacher, said, 'Above all things, be kind. Kindness is the one thing in which we most resemble God and help men. Kindness in mutual relations is the principal charm of life.' It would, perhaps, be better to use the word *love* instead of kindness; for kindness is often mere philanthropy, whereas love is of God. Christ honours friendship.

God as our Friend

Secondly, *we may dare to impute to God the feelings that we impute to our dearest friend.* 'That I might not have sorrow upon sorrow.' Some people are always asking the question, Do you love God? It is far better to dwell on the assurance that God loves you. It is a far more important thing to reckon that God loves you, than for you to try to love God. It is no wonder that people abstain from our places of worship, and go away into sin and worldliness, because the Church has insisted so constantly that they must love God, and they cannot; whereas if the Church would tell people that God loves them, and that they may absolutely reckon on His love, there would be an attraction in the message which would draw them to the Saviour. In God's love they may always dare to impute the very delicacy and tenderness which Paul felt towards Philippi, or Epaphroditus towards his fellow-Christians. **Phil. ii. 19-30**

'And so beside the silent sea
  I wait the muffled oar:
No harm from Him can come to me
  On ocean or on shore.

'I know not where His islands lift
  Their fronded palms in air;
I only know I cannot drift
  Beyond His love and care.'

Always know and believe in the love of God. God is Love; and he that dwelleth in love dwelleth in God, and God in him.

Influence of the Love of God

Thirdly, *the love of God, when it is believed in, makes us very sensitive to other people.* We have our blessed human friendships. From these we rise to conceive of God, and from God we come back to love all men. As with waterfalls, the water dropping from a great height scatters a spray, which makes the stones and boulders array themselves in verdure; so the love of God, falling upon our hearts, will make us very tender towards our fellow-Christians and all men. We must love the suffering and the lost, the loveless and implacable, with something of the love that fills the heart of God, and which never fails. From individuals we rise to God, from God we return to individuals, and from individuals we go forth to the great world.

Love is the only clue to the mysteries of life. As one grows older and knows more, one is more absolutely appalled at the mysteries of sin, and pain, and evil, and there is no clue but to believe that God loves, and that in our turn we must love. St. John says: 'Herein is love made perfect that we may have boldness in the Day of Judgment.' When the worlds crash to ruin, when the universe is in the throes of dissolution, and the eternal certainties are revealed, the only thing which will make the soul strong and unmoved will be the sense that the eternal God has loved it in Christ, and that it has sought to live a life of tender holy love, which it will continue to live for evermore.

If you do not love God, or are not conscious that God loves you, what have you to make you bold in the Day of Judgment? But here stands the Christ Who loves you, Who in love came to die for you, Who by the Spirit is knocking at the door of your heart, Who is pouring out to you a very torrent of love. Have you been disloyal to it? Have you tried its patience to the uttermost? Have you repaid it as Othello did the loving devotion of Desdemona? Ah, will not *your* hell be your remorse, that you thus refused the love of God in Christ? God help you. Believe that God loves you in Christ, and go forth to live a life of perfect love, not causing sorrow upon sorrow, either to Him who loves you so unutterably, or to any other living soul.

15

THE TRUE CIRCUMCISION

Philippians 3:1-3

FINALLY, my brethren, rejoice in the Lord, To write the same things to you, to me indeed *is* not grievous, but for you *it is* safe.
Beware of dogs, beware of evil workers, beware of the concision.
For we are the circumcision, which worship God in the spirit, and rejoice in Christ Jesus, and have no confidence in the flesh.

THERE is a difference of opinion amongst scholars as **Phil. iii. 1-3** to the precise meaning of the Apostle when he wrote this word 'Finally.' Bishop Lightfoot, for instance, supposes that he had already said all that he intended to say, and was bringing his letter to a close. In that case we should accept the alternative rendering, *Farewell!* which is suggested in the margin for *Rejoice.* This would justify the paraphrase: 'And now, my brethren, I must wish you farewell. Rejoice in the Lord.'

It is better, however, to hold that though *Finally* indicates that the Apostle is approaching the end of the Epistle, it is not necessarily a very near approach. (See 1 Thes. iv. 1; 2 Thes. iii. 1.) In this case we might adopt the following paraphrase: 'My letter draws to its close. Its key-note has been the duty of joy, and it shall be so to the end.'

Three Christian duties are enjoined in this brief paragraph: We are to rejoice in the Lord; we are

Phil. iii. 1-3

to beware; and we are to examine ourselves that we be of the true circumcision.

*　　　*　　　*

Christian Joy

THE DUTY OF CHRISTIAN JOY.—The Joy, which is the fruit of the Holy Spirit's work in the heart, coming next to Love, and before Peace, in the enumeration given by the Apostle in Gal. v. 22, is unlike anything which is produced from the natural soil of the heart. It is altogether peculiar to the regenerate soul. It differs from the overflowing good spirits of perfect health, for it persists amid weakness and pain; it differs from mirthful merriment, with its 'quips and cranks,' for it persists in dark hours as well as bright; it differs from mere happiness, for it persists amid the loss of all things. Those who have seen it reflected on the face of God's children will bear witness to the unearthly beauty of expression which it generates. Of this there is a beautiful story told by Dr Trumbull, who describes 'What a boy saw in the face of Adoniram Judson.' One evening, he saw a stranger arrive by train in his native town, whose appearance greatly attracted him. He had never seen such a light on a human face before, and at last it dawned upon him that the man was the great missionary, with whose picture he was familiar. He hurried to summon his own minister, and the little lad was soon forgotten as the two fell into deep conversation; but the boy circled about them, steadfastly looking on that face. Until the day he died, he was accustomed to speak of its beautiful light that shone like the sun. That surely was the reflection of this inner joy.

The True Circumcision

Phil. iii. 1-3

The 'Solar Look'

In the American version of Psalm xxxiv. 5, we read, 'They looked unto Him and were *radiant.*' The 'solar look' is a well-known expression for the smile that shone on the face of Rowlands of Llangeitho; and Margaret Fuller in her diary says, 'Emerson came into our house this morning with a sunbeam in his face.' Nothing more certainly indicates that we have fellowship with God than the radiance of that joy in our step, bearing, and look. The joy of the Lord arises from leaving all our burdens at His feet; from believing that He has forgiven the past as absolutely as the tide obliterates children's writing in the sand; that nothing can come which He does not appoint or permit; that He is doing all things as wisely and kindly as possible; that in Him we have been lifted out of the realm of sin, sorrow, and death into a region of Divine light and love; that we have already commenced the eternal life, and that before us for ever, there is a fellowship with Him so rapturous and exalting that human language can only describe it as unspeakable.

A Thing to be Cultivated

It is a duty for us to cultivate this joy. We must steadfastly arrest any tendency to murmur and complain; to find fault with God's dealings; or to seek to elicit sympathy. We must as much resist the temptation to depression and melancholy as we would to any form of sin. We must insist on watching the one patch of blue in the dark sky, sure that presently it will overspread the Heavens. We must rest upon the promises of God in certain faith that He will triumph gloriously, and that the future will absolutely vindicate the long story of human

Phil. iii. 1-3

pain. We must cultivate a cheery optimism, and an undaunted hope. We must resolve to imitate him, of whom the poet sings, that he—

> 'Never turned his back, but marched breast forward,
> Never doubted clouds would break,
> Never dreamed, though right were worsted, wrong would triumph,
> Held we fall to rise, are baffled to fight better,
> Sleep to wake.'

Rejoicing in the Lord

Moreover, we are to rejoice 'in the Lord.' 'In His presence is fulness of joy, and at His right hand there are pleasures for evermore.' We need not relegate the fulfilment of these sweet words to the far future, but now and here, as we live in fellowship with Him, we shall discover that Christ's presence, made real to us by the Holy Spirit, is the 'deep, sweet well of joy.' We may not be able to rejoice in our circumstances, friends, or prospects, but we can always rejoice in Jesus Christ, whose Nature is the key to the understanding and unlocking of all mysteries, the Well-spring of hope, the Day-star in our hearts, till 'the morning breaks and the shadows flee away.'

It is not difficult to be bright and gay amongst comparative strangers and friends, but often those who are at their best in the social circle, are depressed and taciturn with the immediate inmates of their homes. Does not the wife sometimes shyly confess to herself the wish that her husband might shed the same genial warmth on the breakfast-table, when they are together, as he did on the social circle of the previous evening? But surely, if there is one company in all the world where one should over abound with joy, it is among those to whom our face is as the sun. If it is clouded, shadows fall on all things, if it shines with unobscured beauty, all things partake of a new radiancy. **Phil. iii. 1-3**

Do not be afraid of Joy

'Thou shalt rejoice in all the good which the Lord thy God giveth thee'; 'Every creature of God is good, and nothing to be refused, if it be received with thanksgiving.' God is always putting into our lives bright and blessed things to be used for Him. Do not think it necessary to introduce thorns to your roses, and clouds for the unflecked blue sky. God loves to see His children glad, and so long as you are able to look up from the joy that fills your heart to Him who gave it, connecting the gift with the Giver, there is no reason why you should not drink to the full every cup of blessing which He places in your hand.

We shall hear the Apostle returning to this injunction in iv. 4. To quote his own words, 'To write the same things to you, to me indeed is not irksome, but for you it is safe.' Apparently, he was constantly exhorting them to Christian joy, he was repeating the advice he had often given, laying stress where he had often laid it, with him it was 'precept upon precept, line upon line,' and the teacher who reaffirms and repeats is sure to win in the end.

* * *

The Duty of Taking Heed

Beware of Dogs

'*Beware of dogs.*' Amongst the Ancients, dogs stood as representatives of certain human qualities. For the *Greek*, they stood for ferocity, impudence, greediness; for the *Jew*, for degradation and unclean-

Phil. iii. 1-3

ness. In the Apocalypse the term is applied to those who are destitute of moral qualifications for entering the New Jerusalem—'Without are the dogs, and the sorcerers, and the fornicators, and the idolaters, and everyone that loveth and maketh a lie.' Every traveller in the East knows how herds of dogs prowl through the streets, each pack holding its own street against all comers; they have neither homes nor owners, feeding on the refuse of the streets, quarrelling amongst themselves, and attacking the passers-by.

We are bidden, therefore, to beware of men of a quarrelsome and contentious spirit, who under the guise of religion hide impure and unclean things; and who are not only defiled, but defiling in their influence. If, in our circle of friends, there is one whose influence lowers the tone of our own life, who suggests and arouses thoughts and desires that tend to the gratification of the flesh, the tendency of whose conversation is towards the kitchen of our lower nature, rather than to the observatory of our spirit life, it is our duty to be carefully on our guard, and, if possible, to break off from familiarity and even acquaintance.

And of Evil Workers

'*Beware of evil workers.*' These are not quite the same as evil doers. They are not set upon doing all the harm they can in the world, but are fanatical, unbalanced, and unable to distinguish between a part and the whole, magnifying some microscopical point in Christianity until it blinds the eye to the symmetry, proportion, and beauty of Heaven's glorious scheme. These people are the 'Cranks' of our Churches; they introduce fads and hobbies; they exaggerate the importance of trifles; they catch up every new theory and vagary, and follow it to the detriment of truth and love. Phil. iii. 1-3

It is impossible to exaggerate the harm that these people do, or the desirability of keeping clear of them, they are the pests of every Christian community they enter; and their influence over young and unwary spirits is in a high degree pernicious. The Apostle tells us that when we speak, we must observe the 'proportion of faith.' No exhortation could be more necessary, and whenever any person makes a hobby of one special aspect of the Gospel, always agitating that one point, exaggerating it, and concentrating upon it an amount of attention that should be evenly diffused over the entire system of truth, let us beware, for such an one, intentionally or not, is an evil worker.

The Concision

Beware of the concision. These years of the Apostle's life were greatly embittered by the antagonism of the Judaising teachers who dogged his steps. They did not deny that Jesus was the Messiah, or that His Gospel was the power of God unto salvation, but they insisted that the Gentile converts could only come to the fulness of Gospel privilege through the Law of Moses; they urged that Gentiles must become Jews before they could be Christians; they asserted that if the new converts were not circumcised after the manner of Moses, they could not be saved (Acts xv. 1). Throughout his whole career, the Apostle offered the most strenuous opposition to these men and their teaching. He went so far as to say that they were traitors to

Phi. iii. 1-3

the highest traditions of the past, and that the rite they insisted on, under such circumstances, and when viewed as a condition of salvation by the Blood of Christ, was only a mutilation and cutting of the flesh. It was not circumcision in the true, deep sense of the term. The distinction lies between the words concision and circumcision, the one 'a cutting,' the other a sacred rite.

Un-authorised Demands

Similarly, in our own time, we must beware of those who say that men must pass through certain outward rites before they can be saved. Still amongst us are to be found teachers and writers, the purport of whose words certainly is that, in addition to faith in our Lord, there must be certain acts of obedience to the institutions of the Church. They demand baptism, attendance at the confessional, and strict obedience to fasts, mortifications, and acts of self-denial, as conditions of salvation. Against all these we must be steadfastly on our guard, because they obscure and belittle the Gospel, and divert men's thoughts from Him who is the only way to the Father.

It is specially difficult to be on our guard against these false teachers, because they approach us under the guise of earnestness, sympathy, and religious sentiment. It is not so difficult to watch against the outwardly profane and rebellious, but the most wary may be snared by the specious appeals of those who seem more religious than themselves. It was therefore that the Apostle feared, in his time, lest by any means, as the serpent beguiled Eve with his subtlety, so the minds of his converts should be corrupted from the simplicity which is in Christ (2 Cor. xi. 3). It is when Satan comes to us as an angel of light that he is most to be dreaded.

Phil. iii. 1-3

Examine Yourselves

THE DUTY OF SELF-EXAMINATION. — The analogue of circumcision in the Christian dispensation is clearly not Baptism, but a 'putting off the body of the sins of the flesh.' We must be circumcised in the 'circumcision of Christ,' *i.e.* in the cutting away of all the energy of our self-life, the placing the grave of Jesus between ourselves and the past, and the rising with Him into a realm of liberty and victory, to which He passed by the door of Resurrection (Col. ii. 11, 12).

Specifically, the Apostle gives us the three notes of the true circumcision, by possessing which, we show ourselves to be the true descendants of Abraham, and in the true line of spiritual heredity and blessing; 'For he is not a Jew which is one outwardly; neither is that circumcision which is outward in the flesh; but he is a Jew which is one inwardly; the circumcision is that of the heart, in the spirit and not in the letter; whose praise is not of men but of God' (Rom. ii. 28, 29).

Is our Worship Right?

Do we belong to this holy category? Are the three credentials on which the Apostle insists evident in us? *Do we worship God in the spirit?* The word translated worship means first to do servant's work, then to do religious service, and sometimes priestly duty. Do we understand what it is to live in the temple of worship, performing every duty as to the Lord? Is our worship, whether in public or private, mechanical in outward posture and routine,

Phil. iii. 1-3

or do we know what it is to worship the Father 'in spirit and in truth,' and 'to be in the Spirit on the Lord's Day?' Do we glory (*exult*) in Christ Jesus? Is He our boast and pride? Is following Him our highest ideal? Is the pursuit of His 'Well-done' our loftiest endeavour?

Is our Confidence Right?

Are we amongst those who put no confidence in the flesh? All through the Epistles the flesh stands for self—the self that seeks to justify itself, that endeavours to sanctify itself, that is always fussily endeavouring to win men for God, but has never learned to be submerged beneath the mighty tide and current of God's Spirit. If your religious life is one of self-effort and self-complacency, you must stand back; it is not for you to handle the priceless pearl; your eyes cannot detect its superlative beauty, excellence, and worth. But let all humble souls, who have nothing in which to glory, save the Cross of our Lord Jesus Christ, who put no confidence in themselves, but wholly rest upon the unmerited grace of God, lift up their faces with exceeding great joy. These are the true children of Abraham.

Jake Parsons

Do we rejoice in Christ Jesus? Dr. James H. Taylor wrote some years ago of the curious old New England character named Jake Parsons. 'The change in his life was notorious, so significant and revolutionary had it been. He lay down to sleep one night an absolutely drunken, worthless wretch, having well-nigh lost his power of speech through his dissipation, loved only by the fragment of the family that was left to him. He woke up the next morning an absolutely changed man. For nearly

forty years after that, he lived a life without blemish **Phil. iii. 1-3**
or spot. Eight years after the change, someone asked him what had produced it. This is the explanation he gave: "That night, Jesus Christ appeared in my sleep. His face, as I saw it, seemed so pure, so lovely, so friendly to me that when I awoke I forgot my old vices, and so loved my Saviour that I could not displease Him. He did not speak to me, He only looked at me; but His look told me that there was hope for me, that I could be forgiven, that I could be purified. I looked at Him, and cried like a child; I felt that I was a vile, miserable, wicked wretch, filthier than a dunghill. I cannot tell how I felt. When I looked at Him I was too happy to be afraid; but when I looked at myself I was too afraid to be happy. I forgot all about rum and tobacco, I was thinking so much about Christ, so pure, so lovely, so beautiful, so friendly." '

One who knew him well, so Dr. Taylor said, wrote: 'For thirty-five years he lived a blameless life, beloved by everybody. On a fine summer morning, my friend writes, the glorious old new creature would crawl out of doors, and seating himself on the grassy bank in front of his humble home, turning his sightless face to the sun to feel its warmth, would say: "The door opened into heaven just a little crack. I shall know Him. He will look just so." So he lived until he fell asleep in Jesus.' God give us grace that till the eternal joy overtakes us as a flood we may live in the joy of a similar vision.

16

SELLING ALL TO BUY THE PEARL

Philippians 3:4-9

THOUGH I might also have confidence in the flesh. If any other man thinketh that he hath whereof he might trust in the flesh, I more:

Circumcised the eighth day, of the stock of Israel, *of* the tribe of Benjamin, an Hebrew of the Hebrews; as touching the law, a Pharisee;

Concerning zeal, persecuting the church; touching the righteousness which is in the law, blameless.

But what things were gain to me, those I counted loss for Christ.

Yea doubtless, and I count all things *but* loss for the excellency of the knowledge of Christ Jesus my Lord: for whom I have suffered the loss of all things, and do count them *but* dung, that I may win Christ,

And be found in Him, not having mine own righteousness, which is of the law, but that which is through the faith of Christ, the righteousness which is of God by faith:

Phil. iii. 4-9

The Pearl of Great Price

IN one of His most exquisite parables, our Saviour depicted a man leaving his house in the morning with a heavy bag of gold, and making his way to the market-place, where pearl-sellers displayed the precious ocean gems. He was seeking goodly pearls, and passed from stall to stall with the eye and touch of the connoisseur; but from each stall he turned away dissatisfied. At last he approached one of the sellers, and saw before him on the tray the most exquisite, perfect, and transparent pearl that his eyes had ever lit on. Asking the price, he discovered that it would take all the pearls he had bought, and all the gold in his pouch, to procure it. On starting, he had meant to get the pearls and keep his house and estate, but he learnt that to win that he must sell even these; and so pearls and gold, home and heritage, were all gladly parted with, that that one most priceless jewel might be his own. And always afterwards, when the purchase was concluded, though he was homeless and solitary, the fact that he had got *that* pearl more than compensated him; he counted all things else but loss. **Phil. iii. 4-9**

When our Lord spoke that marvellously beautiful parable, He must have had Saul of Tarsus in His eye—a man with a rich religious nature, capable of an infinite hunger after God, who passed from one stall to another amid the religions of the world, seeking for the best. But finally, when he came where the gem of heaven and earth and sea, the pearl of great price, lay, translucent and glistening, he gladly sacrificed all he possessed to win it; and in this marvellous paragraph he tells us that he counted all things else as loss and refuse compared with Jesus Christ. Oh, that we may understand the superlative excellence of Jesus, and turn from everything that would divide our heart with Him!

Notice how the Apostle uses the Power of Contrast.—There are many ways by which we set forth the value of any possession. We may speak of its rarity; dilate upon its quality; or we may set it in contrast with things that men value. Let us look upon these contrasts, so enhancing 'the Pearl.'

Phil. iii. 4-9

The Knowledge of Christ and the Practice of Judaism

(1) *He contrasted 'the excellency of the knowledge of Christ Jesus' with the ancient and holy system of Judaism.* The Apostle speaks of Judaism with profound reverence and affection. His was not a profane and irreverent soul, that could speak ruthless words about the holy system which, for so many centuries, had satisfied his forefathers, and which, in his own early life, had been so treasured and dear. He never could forget that the architecture of Judaism had been given by God on Sinai's Mount; that the ritualism of the Tabernacle had been wrought out in the laboratory of the Divine mind; that the breath of God had quivered upon the lips of its prophets, and His fire burnt upon the hearts of its seers. He never could forget the generations of holy souls which in Judaism had found their solace, their inspiration, and their comfort; and therefore, with reverent, loving, and tender words, he spoke about that hoary system. What though the light of evening was now shining upon the hills of Zion! What though, ere long, Jerusalem itself must lie beneath the foot of the invader! Still Judaism was dear to him. But contrasted with Jesus Christ, and with that new view of God that Jesus Christ had brought, in which the veil was torn away, and the soul stood face to face with incarnate Deity, Judaism with all its sacred sanctions was but so much loss.

Christ and Sacramental Grace

(2) *He contrasted the knowledge of Christ, next, with the virtue of sacramental efficacy.* He mentions, first, the sacrament of circumcision. He says: 'Circumcision was administered to me, not in

mature life, as to a Gentile proselyte, but in my infancy. On the eighth day I received the initial rite, the badge of the Jew, the seal of the covenant.' He made much of it. It is right that we should make much of the holy sacraments of our religion. Chiefest amongst our religious memories, treasured with unfeigned delight, are certain great moments when we have sat at the Table of our Lord with His saints, and have feasted high, whilst the tide of holy joy has borne us beyond the shores of earthly delight, to the very bosom of our Saviour. Sacraments have meant much to us, but how much to others! Paul said: Though I value beyond compare the sacraments of Judaism, what are these compared to the living Christ? They are but the empty grave from which He has gone forth; they are but the cerements of the tomb, whilst the living Christ passes along the Easter path. **Phil. iii. 4-9**

Christ and High Birth

(3) *He contrasted the knowledge of the Lord with high pedigree.* To have been circumcised was much, but even if he had been the child of a Jewish proselyte he would have been circumcised the eighth day. It did not prove that he had the pure blood of Abraham flowing through his veins; therefore he says: 'I was born a Hebrew; mine was the stock of Israel, the prince with God; I was of the tribe of Benjamin, from which Saul came, the first king of Israel; and which, amid the general faithlessness, clung still to Judah in maintaining the Temple rites. Moreover, I was a Hebrew of Hebrews; no Gentile blood had ever intermingled in our family.' How good some count it to be able to trace back their

Phil. iii. 4-9

pedigree to the Normans, or to the Saxons who preceded the Conquest. Some such pride might have been the Apostle's. He looked upon Rome, and Babylon, and Greece, but knew his descent lay further back than any. They might boast their splendour, but he came of the man who crossed the Euphrates, and settled in Palestine as the friend of God. In him flowed the blood of Moses, who dared behold God face to face; of Joshua, who bade the sun stand still; of Jeremiah and the prophets. But he cries: Compared to Christ, it is nothing. The soul that has won Him is related to a higher family; has received the title of a nobler lineage; is linked, not with the fathers of saintly piety, but to the everlasting Father, the eternal God, through Jesus Christ, the great Brother Man, who has lifted man into union with God. Compared with Him, high lineage and ancient pedigree are but dross.

Christ in Contrast with Pharisaism

(4) *He contrasted the knowledge of Christ with his membership in a noble order of men.* Before Agrippa he said: 'I lived a Pharisee'; and before the Council he cried: 'I am a Pharisee, and the son of a Pharisee.' He here boasts it again—'As touching the law a Pharisee.' The Pharisee in our time has come to be looked upon as the embodiment of pride, arrogance, and supercilious contempt and scorn; but away back in the history of Israel the Pharisees stood for the purest, strictest morality. They were the maintainers of the Law amid the indifference of their time. They opposed the great parties of the courtly Herodians and of the sceptical Sadducees. What if they made their phylacteries broad! It showed that they reverenced

the very text of the Word of God. What though they built the tombs of the prophets! At least they had reverence for the great past. What though they flaunted an outward piety! At least there was the outward recognition of God. There was much to condemn, but they stood for the unity of the Godhead, the resurrection of the Hereafter, and the strictest interpretation of the law. But Paul said that all this was as nothing to him now; he was prepared to be cast out by the Pharisees, to become an outcast and an alien, and be treated as the offscouring of all things. To have Christ was an infinite compensation, which made all the rest seem but loss. **Phil. iii. 4-9**

Christ in Contrast with Reputation

(5) *He contrasted the knowledge of Christ with his own great reputation*—'As touching zeal, persecuting the Church.' Everybody knew how devoted he was to Judaism, and how intent in uprooting Christianity. Breathing fire and sword, he swept like a tornado through Palestine. The disciples trembled when he came near any city in which they were gathered, for there was every fear that he would drag them before the Councils and commit them to prison. In many cases he ruthlessly stamped out the infant church in blood. There was nothing he would not do, so relentless, so merciless, so unsparing. And with all this, he was building up such a reputation as would have given him prominence in all aftertime in his fatherland and amongst his fellow-countrymen. It is not a small thing for a young man of thirty to build up a reputation like that, because it means high marriage, power, wealth and prestige. It means everything that a man cares for and seeks; but when

Phil. iii. 4-9

Paul stood, with everything of this world alluring him on the one hand, and with Christ on the other calling him to the cross, torture, isolation, poverty, and everything the flesh of man hates, he said: I am married to Christ, and in Him am married to suffering, sorrow, and loss; but I look on it as a man who has made a good bargain—for I have won the Pearl, Christ.

Christ in Contrast with Personal Uprightness

(6) *He contrasted the knowledge of Christ with the satisfaction of blameless character*—'As touching the righteousness which is in the law, found blameless.' There is a tribunal always in session, a tribunal before which we are all constantly being tried; and we ourselves often sit upon that tribunal to try those above us, on our level, and beneath us. But in our quiet hours we leave that judgment-seat, and apply to ourselves the standards which we have been applying to our fellows. At such times we cannot but notice how, compared with many around us, our own character appears blameless and flawless. Thank God, we say, after we have been considering the case of the drunkard, the miser, or the dissipated, we are not as they are. And as we apply to ourselves the standard beneath which so many of our fellows have been condemned, we are disposed to take to ourselves considerable credit. 'I go to church, I pay my subscriptions, I do not drink, I do not indulge the flesh, I keep my tongue in control; my dearest and nearest cannot accuse me of being anything but a loving, tender man; my life is blameless.' Thereupon we conclude that we are right.

These are the people that it is hardest to win for

Christ. They are enclosed and encased within the armour of their self-righteousness; they are so complacent that when the strongest sermons are levelled against congregations they shelter themselves beneath their armour-plate, and say: The sermon is good for others, but it cannot mean us. When a man wakes up suddenly to see that in God's sight all that counts for nothing; when Christ comes to him and casts the X-rays upon his inner life; when he sees the glory of the Great White Throne compared with the linen he has been washing for years with such arduous punctiliousness; when he sees that what he thought to be white and clean is only as filthy as rags to the Son of God, there comes the greatest fight of his life. Many a man would be prepared to give up his church, to renounce his sacraments, to step out from his high family, with its pedigree, and from the blamelessness of his earlier life; many a man would be prepared to sacrifice his reputation for earnestness: but when it comes to saying that his righteousness is but filthy rags; that the boat he has been constructing will not carry him across the mighty deluge of waters; that the tower he has built upon the reef will not resist the autumn storm, in counting even his blamelessness as loss and dross—yea as dung—then there comes the greatest fight.

Phil. iii. 4-9

(7) *He contrasted the knowledge of God's Righteousness which is by faith, with his own righteousness, which was of the law.* In the Epistle to the Romans the Apostle clearly describes the righteousness, which is of the law, 'That the man which doeth these things shall live by them' (Rom. x. 5). The doing of the

Contrasted Righteousness

things prescribed by the Law in the heart, or the Law on the Tables of Stone, has occupied the minds and governed the activities of legalists and ritualists from the beginning of the world. It was this that prompted Luther to fastings and scourgings, beneath which his body was reduced to an extremity, and that encouraged Bunyan to hope that an outward reformation would satisfy the outcry of his conscience. But such men have always found their efforts unavailing. However zealous they may be in going about to establish their own righteousness, men discover that what has seemed a white and flawless robe is only as filthy rags, in the searching light of the great white throne.

But the Righteousness which is 'of God,' because it was designed by His wisdom, and is offered by His unmerited grace, requires no 'going about.' There is no need to say, 'Who shall ascend unto heaven,' or 'Who shall descend into the deep.' 'The word of faith is nigh thee.' Its one condition is the open hand of a faith, that takes what the risen saviour offers. Just as soon as the soul trusts Him—not merely believing *about*, but *in* Him,—in that moment it is clothed upon with the Righteousness of Christ, wrought out by His perfect obedience unto death, which is 'unto all and upon all them that believe' (Rom. iii. 22). It is only necessary to abandon our own righteousness to gain Christ and His righteousness. We cannot have both. But when we have resolved to drop the one, that we may take the other; in making the choice, we suddenly find ourselves in Him, and arrayed in the beauteous dress, Who was made sin for us that we might be made the Righteousness of God (2 Cor. v. 21). Phil. iii. 4-9

Have you come to Him? The time is coming when you will have to be found somewhere. The Apostle says, 'That I may be *found* in Him.' You will have to be found by the swirling tides of sorrow, by some supreme temptation, by the final test of death; you will have to be found in the Judgment; you will have to be found in the dissolution of the Heavens and the Earth. When God comes to find you, where will you be found? In the cardboard of your own goodness, or in the completed Righteousness of Jesus Christ, which He wrought out on the Cross in tears and blood, and which is yours directly you look with penitent trust towards Him? God grant that when you are found, it may be with the Pearl of great price in your hand, and with the Righteousness of Jesus Christ upon your soul!

17

THE SOUL'S QUEST

Philippians 3:10,11

THAT I may know Him, and the power of His resurrection, and the fellowship of His sufferings, being made conformable unto His death;

If by any means I might attain unto the resurrection of the dead.

Phil. iii. 10, 11

THE Apostle in these wonderful verses twice uses the word Resurrection; and surely we must interpret it by his well-known teaching, in which he speaks of Christ's Resurrection as primarily affecting spiritual experience. In Romans vi. and Colossians ii. and iii., he is not dealing with the resurrection of the body, but with that entrance into a higher state of thought and experience which centres around the risen Lord.

Paul and the Resurrection of the Body

It is impossible to suppose that the Apostle had any doubt as to the resurrection of his body, whether at the coming of the Lord or afterwards. Surely it could never have entered into his mind that any excellence in Christian attainment could affect his sharing with the saints in the first resurrection, when suddenly, 'in the twinkling of an eye,' the great transformation will come to those who are alive and remain, whilst resurrection will come to those who have fallen asleep. The fact that he belonged to Christ, was a member of His mystical Body, and had given evidence of the depth and sincerity of his conversion, was enough to secure his enjoyment in the privileges of the first resurrection, altogether apart from the renunciations which he had described in the foregoing paragraph. Clearly then, the resurrection of the verses before us has to do with the life hidden with Christ in God, in whom we died indeed unto the world and sin, and are alive unto God through Jesus Christ. Phil. iii. 10, 11

We have already seen that Paul was willing to 'count all things but loss for the excellency of the knowledge of Christ Jesus my Lord.' Here he strikes that note again, and says that he counts all things but loss if only he may win Christ. In one of his quaint poems, Quarles tells us how he loves the earth, the air, the sea, and the heavens. He calls them 'the spangled suburbs of the celestial city'; but they cannot give him a satisfaction in which he can rest, and he has to strike through all these outward facts and forms to arrive at God and see them in Him.

> 'In having all things, and not Thee, what have I?
> Not having Thee, what have my labours got?
> Let me enjoy but Thee, what further crave I?
> And having Thee alone what have I not?
> I wish nor sea, nor land, nor would I be
> Possessed of heaven, if heaven unpossessed Thee.'

Such thoughts must have been in the Apostle's mind, enabling him to make nothing of his losses, and everything of his gains, when he turned from the world, its joys and hopes, its religion and righteousness, to Jesus Christ—'his exceeding Joy.'

Phil. iii. 10, 11

Let us consider the soul's quest for *the personal Christ*; for *the power of His Resurrection*; for *the fellowship of His sufferings*; for *the likeness of His risen glory.*

The Soul's Quest for the Personal Christ

'That I may know Him.' We cannot be put off by a doctrine about Christ, or by the Book which from end to end speaks of Christ, or with a hearsay or second-rate knowledge of Christ, we need to press through all these ante-rooms, passing from one to another, to stand in the personal presence of the Living Saviour. This is the prerogative of all holy souls; they are permitted not simply to know about Him, but to know Him, not only to read of His excellency and beauty in the Book that is fragrant with the myrrh, aloes, and cassia of His presence, but to have fellowship with the Apostles, who saw, heard, beheld, and handled the Word of Life.

This is the heart and essence of Christianity. Other religions are content with ornate rites, an elaborate priesthood, an intricate system of doctrine and regulations, but the Christian, taught by the Holy Spirit, refuses to rest in any of these, and in comparison with the Master counts them as so much refuse.

We may know Him personally, intimately, face to face. Christ does not live back in the centuries, nor amid the clouds of heaven: He is near us, with us, compassing our path and our lying down, and acquainted with all our ways. But we cannot know Him in this mortal life except through the illumination and teaching of the Holy Spirit. Let us ask Him to shed His clear beams on the face of Jesus, so that it shall haunt our day-dreams and our nights. Phil. iii. 10, 11

We must not rest until we 'Know Him'

We should never rest until we know Him as we know our friend, and are able to read without speech the movements of His soul. We should know by a quick intuition what will please and what will hurt His pure and holy nature. We should know where to find Him; should be familiar with His modes of thought and methods of action; should understand and identify ourselves with His goings forth, as, day by day, He goes through the world healing and saving. What a difference there is between the knowledge which the man in the street has of some public character and that which is vouchsafed to the inner circle of his home; and we must surely know Christ, not as a stranger who turns in to visit for the night, or as the exalted King of men,—there must be the inner knowledge as of those whom He counts His own familiar friends, whom He trusts with His secrets, who eat with Him of His bread (Psalm xli. 9).

To know Christ in the storm of battle; to know Him in the valley of shadow; to know Him when the solar light irradiates our faces, or when they are darkened with disappointment and sorrow; to know the sweetness of his dealing with bruised reeds and smoking flax; to know the tenderness of His sympathy and the strength of His right hand—all this involves many varieties of experience on our part, but each of them, like the facets of a diamond, will reflect the prismatic beauty of His glory from a new angle.

Phil. iii. 10, 11

The Soul's Quest for the Power of His Resurrection

The Risen Christ is full of all authority and power. We remember the two mountains of His life,—the one at the beginning, the other at the end. On the first, Satan offered Him the authority and glory of the world, if only He would perform one act of homage, and so evade the experiences of the Cross and grave. It was as though he said, 'Son of God, if Thou wilt do homage to me, Thou needest not sweat the bloody sweat of Gethsemane, or undergo the scourging of Gabbatha, or the shame of Calvary.' But the Lord would not heed the suggestion, but descended the rugged valley path, passed by way of the Cross to the glory; and was therefore able on the other mountain —that of the Ascension—to say 'All power (authority) is given to Me in heaven and upon earth.'

Addressing the beloved apostle, some years after, Jesus said, 'I am the First and the Last, and the Living One,' *there* was His Life in its perennial and Divine fountain,—'I became dead, and behold, I am alive for evermore,' *there* was His Life in its victory over death,—'and have the keys of death and the unseen world,' *there* is Life regnant over all the unseen spaces and powers. As the waters of a river, passing through various soils, take up into themselves the quality of each, so the life of Christ in its human aspect, passing through the successive scenes of His earthly ministry, acquired qualities with which it stands possessed for ever. Listen to His glorious words—'Be of good cheer, I have overcome . . . ' 'To him that overcometh will I give to sit with Me in My throne, as I also overcame and sat down with My Father in His throne.'

Phil. iii. 10, 11

Power from the Risen Lord

What power emanates from the Risen Christ! He is the Divine storage of eternal and solar forces. 'In Him all fulness dwells.' An electric battery just charged, is not fuller of dynamic energy than Christ is of æonial and resurrection power; and directly the soul is united to Him by a living faith, it is as when we touch a battery with our hand, and its stored forces begin to thrill our body. This is what the Apostle meant when he spoke about the 'power of His Resurrection.' He meant that to the believing soul, the power of the life which resides in Christ pours into the receptive spirit, forthwith it rises from the grave of passion in which it had been imprisoned, escapes from the bondage of corruption by which it was held, and goes forth into the glorious liberty of the sons of God. Just as the Christ could not be holden by the bands of death, so the soul which trusts Him is emancipated, enthused, raised into an altogether new atmosphere, breathes the ozone of eternity, is thrilled by the powers of the unseen, and meets all appeals from the lower world with an abundance of life, which is impervious to disease, infirmity, and temptation. Just as a really healthy life may pass through microbes of disease, which would effect the overthrow of less vigorous and buoyant health, so the soul which is infilled with the Resurrection power of Christ, is more than a conqueror in the midst of the most virulent temptation, whether arising from its own heredity or the combined power of the pit.

* * *

Phil. iii. 10, 11

The Quest of the Soul for the Fellowship of Christ's Sufferings

Notice the Apostle's order. He does not put the fellowship of Christ's sufferings as the first thing which the soul must seek; he does not expect that we should go about the world making death and the grave our main goal and object. His doctrine is healthier far. He says, Seek to know the Risen Lord, open your hearts to Him that the power of His resurrection life may enter and infill, and in the fulness of your joy you will not stay to count the cost of having fellowship with His sufferings. The experience of suffering will, so to speak, be forgotten in the radiancy of your exultation. As the pain of the woman in travail is forgotten amid the joy of bearing a child into the world, so will the keenest suffering seem but a pin-prick compared with the eternal weight of glory.

Often Christian people go through the world with a lugubrious expression on the face, much as some ancient ascetic would have done, as though looking for their graves. It is far better to tread the pathways of life, seeking to know the power of the Risen Life, for when that is within, it counts all things but loss, and even death a gain.

Conditions of the Risen Life

It is inevitable that if we are to know much of Christ's Resurrection, and in proportion as we know it, we shall drink of the cup of His sufferings. Every step further into the Risen Life will involve some deeper and more poignant pang of pain. Men will misunderstand us, as they misunderstood Him, men will drop away from us and leave us alone, as they left Him, we shall be compelled to stand in the pillory of hatred and rejection. To be received by

Christ into His secret, will necessarily secure our exclusion from the familiar intercourse of the world; to stand with Him in the height, will have its counterpart in our being thrust down into the depth; to have fellowship under the open heaven of God, with the voice of the Father, and the descending Dove, will certainly involve the being driven into the wilderness to meet the full brunt of temptation. But the soul that really loves Christ will not shrink from the ordeal, it will be glad to enter into His sufferings, because it realises that to know these is to know Him, and that the very distance into which the meteor is driven in the darkness, is in proportion to the close proximity and length of its fellowship with the sun that attracts it into its inner circle. **Phil. iii. 10, 11**

Baxter said in this connection: 'A cheap religion is not usually accompanied with any notable degree of comfort. Although the person be a sincere-hearted Christian, he cannot have much peace or joy. A confirmed Christian is one that taketh self-denial for one half of his religion.' How true this is! and it is absolutely certain that you may judge your heights by your depths, and gauge the amount of Resurrection Power which is within you by the depths of your sympathy with, and understanding of, the Cross of Christ. You may doubt indeed if you have been admitted into the fulness of the one, unless you have gone down into the depths of the other.

The Soul's Quest after the Attainment of the Resurrection Life

The Risen Life involves the recognition of all human interests, the loving reciprocity of friendship and comradeship, the fulfilment of all the duties that devolve upon us, though performing them all from

Phil. iii. 10, 11

another standpoint. The Risen Lord called Mary by the familiar name, sat in the social circle with the beloved band of His apostles, went forth to minister to their physical needs,—as on the morning when He prepared fish and bread for them,—stood up from His throne in vivid sympathy with the martyr who was being stoned to his death, and came to encourage the disciple who wrought in the mines of Patmos. But there was a difference in it all. He came from another sphere to succour them. So it will be with us; the Resurrection life does not mean that we are indifferent to any human tie or call, but that we have laid hold of a new source of power by which it may be fulfilled. Our life is no longer fitful, with the spasmodic energy of our own impulse, but fed from the perennial fountains of Christ's life. Because He lives we live also; His life constrains us; His Spirit fills us; we are already in the heavenlies even as He was (John iii. 13).

We utilise the forces of a higher plane of being than that which other men can utilise. Discoverers, from Archimedes to Edison, may use the physical forces of the unseen. Christian science may employ its psychical forces, but we touch those spiritual forces which are resident in the Holy Spirit, and with which the nature of the Risen Lord is replete. Just as there is a distinction between the civilised man and the savage, because the former is able to use those mighty energies of which the untutored child of nature knows nothing, so there is a great difference between the man who has entered into the power of Christ's Resurrection and other men.

As electricity is a higher form of power than that of water or gas, so the Christian who lives in union with the Risen Christ is able to exert a higher form of power than others. He knows the secrets of God, and obeys the laws of a life which is far removed from that which he used to live. Through death to his self-life, he has commenced to use the power of the Eternal Word, 'Who was, and is, and is to come.' Phil. iii. 10, 11

18

APPREHENDED TO APPREHEND

Philippians 3:12

NOT as though I had already attained, either were already perfect: but I follow after, if that I may apprehend that for which also I am apprehended of Christ Jesus.

Phil. iii. 12

WE may compare these words with those which the Apostle uttered in the presence of Agrippa: 'Wherefore, O king Agrippa, I was not disobedient unto the heavenly vision.' That vision included his appointment to be a minister and a witness of all the things which he had seen, and of those in which fresh revelations were to be made, the promise of deliverance from the people and the Gentiles, and the prevision of the marvellous results that would accrue from his testimony to the Gentiles (Acts xxvi.16-18).

With these words to help us we can better understand the purport of this striking phrase.

* * *

Paul apprehended of Christ Jesus

PAUL REALISED THAT HIS CONVERSION HAD BEEN HIS APPREHENSION BY GOD.—To hear some men speak you would suppose that the initiative in their religious life had come from themselves, that the first approaches towards God emanated from their own hearts, that they were independent of Him until they voluntarily put themselves within the range of His care and help. Nothing could be further from the truth. As well might the flower speak of discovering the sunshine and turning its face thitherwards. The initiative of the religious life does not come from man but from God. The first steps in reconciliation are not on our side but on His. If we seek God it is only because He has been seeking us from early childhood, and has contrived the span of our life and the location of our home with special reference to our feeling after Him and finding Him (Acts xvii. 26, 27). **Phil. iii. 12**

God's Love realised in Conversion

When a man turns to God, the first thing he realises is that throughout the wild wanderings of his youth, and amid all the fret and war of his manhood, even when he has been most stubborn and rebellious, God's love has never ceased to seek him. The true comparison for the soul is not that it is immured in dark galleries and catacombs, out of which it presently seeks to escape, but that God comes into the intricacies of its rebellion and wandering, calling tenderly and earnestly, awakening it from its stupefaction, shedding on fast-closed eyes beams of light to startle the drowsy sleeper, and eliciting by every method in his power a quick response. We love because we were first loved; we seek because we were sought; we leave our far country, not only because hunger impels, but because frequent missives from our Father's house tell us that He cannot be at rest until we are again seated at His table.

As it was by Paul

Paul realised that from his earliest hour, God had been about his path and his ways. When he was circumcised the eighth day, when he was brought up as a son of the law, when he was engaged in perse-

Phil. iii. 12

cuting the Church, when he was working out for himself a righteousness in which to stand the searching inspection of the great White Throne, in and through all the Spirit of God had been near, teaching, admonishing, and stimulating his quest for the Pearl of great price. Finally, he recognised that on the day, ever memorable, of his journey to Damascus, the love of God in the Person of Christ had apprehended or seized upon him.

After all, is not this conversion? We grasp the hand of Christ because He has grasped ours, we are apprehended to live after the highest and noblest ideals because His hand has been laid upon us in arrest.

When Christ apprehends us it is for a Great Purpose

'That I may apprehend that for which also I was apprehended by Christ Jesus.' When God brings us to Himself, it is to realise some lofty ideal on which He has set His heart. In some cases, the eye beholds, as Moses did in vision, the tabernacle which it is to build, it stands in clearly defined outlines, with every knop and tassel, every curtain and fringe, every pillar and hook perfectly designed. In other cases, the pattern is only revealed step by step and day by day. Each morning the Spirit of God presents to us in the circumstances of our life, and in the impulse of our heart, some new item in the great conception, and calls on us to fulfil it,—thus the temple *groweth* into a dwelling place for the Eternal.

Whichever method God may adopt with you, whether in the early morning of life you stand upon the mountain and see the completed plan, or your eyes are holden so that you are permitted to see it only by piecemeal, yet be sure that there was a great thought in His heart when He drew you out of the horrible pit and from the miry clay, and set your feet upon a rock, and established your goings. Phil. iii. 12

We must not refuse to apprehend that for which Christ apprehended us

In all life there ought to be the human response to the Divine call. We do not become saints against our will or in violation to our free agency. We must be workers together with God, working out what He works in. We must first see something of the goal to which our steps are to be directed, and then we must mount up with wings as eagles, run without being weary, walk without being faint. It is possible for each of us to turn our backs upon the heavenly vision, shut our ears to the Divine call, and take the downward course. The poet Dante caps his description of the rich young man who went away sorrowful, by calling it *The Great Refusal.* Herod and Pilate, Felix and Agrippa, all refused to apprehend that for which they were apprehended, and their course has been followed by myriads.

The Case of John Stuart Mill

There is a modern instance in the biography of John Stuart Mill, aptly quoted by Dr. W. M. Taylor in this connection. These are his words: 'I was in a dull state of nerves, such as everybody is occasionally liable to, unsusceptible to enjoyment or pleasureable excitement—one of those moods when what is pleasure at other times becomes insipid or indifferent—the state, I should think, in which converts to Methodism usually are, when smitten by their first conviction of sin. In this frame of mind it

Phil. iii. 12

occurred to me to put the question directly to myself: "Suppose that all your objects in life were realised; that all the changes that you are looking forward to could be completely effected at this very instant, would this be a great joy and happiness to you?" and an irrepressible self-consciousness distinctly answered, *No.* At this my heart sank within me; the whole foundation on which my life was constructed fell down, all my happiness was to have been found in the continual pursuit of this end, the end that ceased to charm, and how could there ever again be any interest in the means? I seemed to have nothing left to live for.' But, when earthly projects fell down, did not the Lord draw near, laying on him His arresting hand, and beseeching him to adopt a more stable foundation for his life? And is it not clear that he too made a great and deliberate refusal to feel after God if haply he might find Him, who is not far from any one of us?

We must not be content with a Partial Attainment

'Not as though I had already attained, either were already perfect.' And again, 'Brethren, I count not myself to have apprehended.' As Paul looked at the result of his work, the large cities which had become permeated with Christian truth, the flourishing Churches which looked to him as their founder, the Epistles which he had written, and the commanding influence of his spoken words, surely he might have counted himself to have apprehended. He did not do so because as he drew nearer to the attainment of God's ideal, some new phase opened, as when we are climbing the hills, and having reached the vantage-ground on which our eyes have been set during hours of arduous toil, we see another height rising beyond. Phil. iii. 12 The more the glory shone on the face of Moses, the quicker he was to veil it from view; the higher the soul rises into likeness with Christ, the deeper its humility. When we see what Christ is in the glory of His Person, and in the greatness of His love, we feel that our own attainments are as molehills to Alps.

A friend discovered Thorwaldsen in tears, and on asking why the distinguished sculptor was giving way to depression, he received this reply, 'Look at that statue. I have realised my ideal, and therefore fear that I have reached the high-water mark of my profession. When a man is satisfied, he ceases to grow.'

It is also said that Tennyson was seventeen years in writing 'In Memoriam.' He wrote the little song 'Come into the Garden, Maud' fifty times before he gave it to the public. The wife of a distinguished painter said, 'I never saw my husband satisfied with one of his productions.' Thus self-dissatisfaction lies at the root of our noblest achievements.

There is no condition of growth in the Divine life so necessary as a deep sense of dissatisfaction for the past. Let us admit that we have not attained to that identification with the Death of Christ, with His Resurrection, or with the gift of Pentecost, to that deliverance from the power of sin, and that conformity to His perfect image to which we have been called with a heavenly calling. Even if we are kept from known and outward sin, how much shortcoming

Phil. iii.

there is in our hearts. If we have ceased doing the things that we ought not to do, alas for us, there are so many things that we fail to do.

Paul not discouraged though he had not fully apprehended

He knew Him whom he had believed, and therefore he said, 'I press on toward the goal.' Depression, which makes us slacken our steps, is from below, humility, which makes us more eager to attain God's purpose, is from above. Never yield to discouragement, never sit down face to face with failure or imperfection as though these were a necessary part of your life. God can forgive failure, but He cannot forgive those who abandon their high quest, and allow their hands to hang down and their knees to fail. Grasp the banner again, young soldier, and rush forward into the fight. Let past failure be an incentive to more commanding achievements. Remember that Christ is always just in front; His grace is sufficient; dare to claim the fulfilment of His own promise, 'My grace is sufficient for thee.'

It seems as though these words of Paul are characteristic of his eager spirit through all the ages. Not only did he press on through obloquy and reproach, through imprisonment and threatened death; but from the excellent glory into which he has passed, we seem to hear those same clarion notes, 'I press on.' Pressing on in the knowledge of God, pressing on in high and noble service, pressing on only a few steps behind the Lamb as He goes ever conquering and to conquer, pressing on until the pulling down of all rule and authority and power has been accomplished, and God has become all in all.

19

'ONWARDS AND UPWARDS'

Philippians 3:13,14

BRETHREN, I count not myself to have apprehended; but *this* one thing *I do*, forgetting those things which are behind, and reaching forth unto those things which are before,

I press toward the mark for the prize of the high calling of God in Christ Jesus.

Phil. iii. 13, 14

The Divine Call

THAT word *calling* frequently occurs in the Epistles—'Ye see your calling brethren, how that not many wise, not many mighty, are *called*.' And again, 'That ye may know what is the hope of His *calling*'—the hope to which He calls you. And again, 'Who hath *called* us with a holy calling.' And again, 'Partakers of a heavenly calling.' And again, 'Ye were *called* in one hope of your calling'—to which we have been called in the unity of the Spirit. The wireless telegraphy of God's Spirit is ever bringing the Divine call to every soul. It is circling around you in the tremulous vibrating air. If only your ears were attuned to it, you would detect the low sweet voice of God, nearer, clearer, stronger, intenser, more thrilling, more eager. The voice of God calls, calls *you*.

* * *

The Glory to which God calls

To what goal does God beckon us, with the prize glittering in the sunlight above it, held before us by

Phil. iii. 13, 14

the pierced Hand? What is God's goal and mark? The Apostle, in his early life, was bent on becoming a Rabban, one of the elders of the people, the chief of the Pharisee party. He was filled with ideals and hopes, which he had long revolved in his eager mind; but as his palfrey bore him towards Damascus, suddenly he beheld an ideal, presented to him in the person of Jesus of Nazareth, before which all the former ones paled in their beauty, as the morning star pales before the sunrise. He saw the hollowness of being merely a Pharisee; the formality, the externalism, the inadequacy of the desire which had hitherto inspired his nature. Forthwith he became inspired with a new purpose, and set himself to aim at the spotless loveliness, the ideal of strength, sweetness, might, mercy, purity and gentleness combined in the character of Jesus, so that from that moment he cried, 'I surrender everything; my hopes, aims, ambitions, ideals—I cast them all away, as a man casts dross, and till I die, it shall be my passionate desire to realise in my own character, day by day, something of the beauty and glory which I have seen upon the face of the Man of Nazareth. This one thing I do: I press toward the mark for the prize of the high calling of God.'

God's Call to you

God's voice is calling you to-day to that, to be like Jesus; to know Him, to love Him better, to resemble Him more completely, to strike off from your character a little more of the encompassing stone, and to bring out some new line and lineament of the perfect statue.

Phil. iii. 13, 14

It is a High Calling

It is a *high calling* because it comes from above, from God; the conception of it has emanated from His heart. It is a *high calling* because it is worthy of God. It is a *high calling* because it is so much above the ideals of men. Men strive to get money, forgetting that there are no pockets in a shroud; seek for pleasure, forgetting that the pleasures of this world are like the snow upon the river, 'a moment white, then gone for ever'; strive after fame and supremacy, forgetting that there must come a moment when their remains will lie beneath the pall on which the crown and sceptre of empire rest, to be assumed by another. When once the eye has caught sight of this vision, it is attracted by a light above the brightness of the sun of wealth, above the brightness of the sun of fame, above the brightness of the sun of rank, above the brightness of the sun of worldly power. The lofty ideal glistens before each of us of becoming like our Master, knowing Him, feeling the power and fascination of His resurrection, tasting the fellowship of His sufferings, and being conformed to Him in His death, rising day by day higher and nearer to Him in His royal beauty, the Divine Man, God's ideal for us all.

A Calling above our Aspirations

It is also a *high calling* because always above our highest aspirations. How touching is that story told already of the great sculptor, who, after years of work, achieved a statue so perfectly fashioned that he could discover no line that needed to be retouched, no feature that needed to be remodelled. It stood there in absolute beauty, and a friend found

Phil. iii. 13, 14

him in tears beside it, as he said, 'I shall never do anything better than that, it is the consummation of my ideal.' Thank God, we may follow after the perfect beauty of Christ for untold ages, but shall never be found weeping because there are no more worlds to conquer. There will always be a new Alp rising above Alp, a beautiful and more beautiful conception calling us to leave that which we have already attained.

A Calling that summons us Heavenwards

And then this is a *high calling* because it summons us to where Christ sits at the right hand of God. It compels us to look upward, and set our affections upon things above, not in things on the earth. 'Alas,' you say, 'it is too great for me; remember what I am, poor dust and ashes, full of failure and infirmity; I have so often tried and succumbed; there can be no possible hope for me to realise it; it is but a mockery to incite me to this great quest.' But remember, Paul started from a lower level than yours; he was a blasphemer, and had trampled under foot the Blood of Jesus. Remember also that this high calling is 'in Christ,' and if you are in Christ, you have got your foot upon the first rung of the ladder, upon the first step of the staircase. It is 'in Christ.' You cannot be in Christ without having Christ in you; and God has put the Spirit of His Son within you that you may evolve what is involved. God has consigned to your keeping His Beloved, that hour by hour you may strike away that which is of self and sin, that the beauty of Jesus Christ may become more conspicuous before the eyes of men.

'Onwards and Upwards'

* * * Phil. iii. 13, 14

(1) 'This *one thing* I do.' The Apostle says we must be discontented with what we have attained, and intent on the one goal which lies before us. None of us can doubt that success in life is not attained by genius, but plodding industry. A man may be swift as Asahel, of fleetest foot, but if he does not set his mind upon a distinct goal he will be outstripped by a man of slower foot, but more resolute purpose. It is not the hare that runs and sleeps, but the tortoise that plods on towards a determined point that wins the race. It is so in business, in art, in war, and in love.

How this Ideal may be Realised

Abundant Help

Many men are born into the world who are clever at a number of things, but succeed in nothing. There are others who concentrate their minds upon one thing and succeed, though they have not half the genius of their competitors. And 'the one thing' we must set our minds upon, and pursue with unremitting diligence, is God's ideal presented to us in Jesus Christ. And it is good to know that every incident in life may be made to conduce to our high purpose. As the bee will get honey from a thousand different flowers, so we can accumulate the honey of a holy character from every flower in the garden of our life. Every circumstance may be pressed into our service for the attainment of a more Christ-like character.

The votary of pleasure must sometimes retire from the giddy whirl of amusement, to recruit exhausted energies. A London season only lasts for two or three months, and then the fashionable world must

Phil. iii. 13, 14

go to the country, or the seaside resort, to recuperate. The business man who never gets relief from its pressure will be unable to hold his own against commercial competition. So with the student; he works up for the examination, straining every nerve for it, and then lays aside his studies and goes off to mountain or shore.

Are our circumstances co-operating?

But everything in life may help you to be like Christ! In your moments of solitude you will most easily make headway; but the hours of conflict and temptation will be the times in which you will be able to achieve most of the likeness of Christ. When you lose the harvest of your toils; when the tongue of slander detracts from your good name; when you have to bear, day after day, the scornful and averted look of your fellows; when all your life is overcast by the shadow of death, and you have no more heart to live; in days of discouragement and disappointment spent in the solitude of your chamber; in days when you sit in the darkened room, where the beloved one is slowly passing from your embrace, and the precious life is ebbing from the heart drop by drop—in all these times, when you are made aware of something which is not as sweet, or beautiful, as it might be, you may take the opportunity of becoming more perfectly fashioned towards the likeness of your Lord.

The men who do one thing in the world are bound to succeed. Remember the story of the greatest of orators, Demosthenes, who set himself resolutely to cure a defect in his speech, by speaking, with pebbles in his mouth, against the roar of the sea. Men who are able to bend themselves upon one thing must be successful in its achievement. Oh, that we may say: 'Come weal, come woe, prosperity or disappointment, sunshine or shadow, we will never rest, day nor night, but press towards the mark of increasing likeness to Christ, that men may be reminded in us of Him!' Phil. iii. 13, 14

The Duty of Forgetting

(2) If we would press on, we must *learn to forget.* We are all tempted to live in the past, to look up at the fading laurels which we have gained, as though they could never be equalled or surpassed; to say, 'We shall never do anything so good as that again, never be able to reach quite so high, or realise quite so much; to paint so fair a picture, to execute so beautiful a statue.' This is fatal. Never rest upon your past attainments; forget them. Forget the rapture of your first communion; the earliest addresses and sermons, which you used to feed and rest upon; the trophies which attended your earliest efforts; do not quote these things as your highest; do not look back, lest, like Lot's wife, you be petrified, and unable to advance.

Forget the innocence of your childhood. Do not say with Hood—

> 'I remember, I remember,
> The house where I was born,'

and end by lamenting that you were nearer heaven when a boy than you are now. Innocence is good, but purity is better. The breath of a child's sleep is fragrant and soft; but give me the deep slumber of the man who rests after a well-fought field. Not

Phil. iii. 13, 14

untempted innocence, but the strength which comes of victorious conflict should be our aim.

No morbid dwelling on the Sinful Past

And do not dwell upon past sin. When a new boy comes to the philanthropist, a boy who has seen and known sin enough to blight his life for ever, the wise philanthropist says, 'My boy, I want you to forget the past.' He fits him out with new clothes, and tries to wipe out the memory of the degrading sins in which he has played a part. And the boy breaks from his past, and steps up into an entirely new life under that fostering care.

Remember God's Pardon

There may be things in our past of which we are ashamed, which might haunt us, which might cut the sinews of our strength. But if we have handed them over to God in confession and faith, He has put them away and forgotten them. Forget them, and, leaving the past attainments, the innocence of childhood, and the sin which has vitiated and blackened your record, reach forward to realise the beauty of Jesus. Do not be content with anything less. But it is important never to allow the imperfect and second-best to pass unconfessed. Too often we have done it, whispering: 'Yes, I have failed, let it pass'; instead of confessing to God and man, and crying: 'Never more; I *will* be Christlike, I *will* be pure with the purity of Jesus, I will be tender, sweet, and gentle as Christ was. My God, I hear Thee calling; I hear Thee calling, I will arise; Excelsior, excelsior, I will climb. Never a day shall pass that does not see some added beauty of Christ to my heart and life, through the power of Thy Holy Spirit.'

‘Onwards and Upwards’

‘I press toward the mark for the prize.’ What? Heaven? No, Heaven has been won by the merits of the Lord Jesus. A throne? A crown? No, for these are the gifts of free grace. What, then, is the prize?

Phil. iii. 13, 14

There is a Prize

God calls us to the goal, but there is a prize beyond and in addition to the goal. What? Blessedness! To be Christlike is to be blessed. When we have overcome some temptation there has been such a sense of blessedness. When we have gone through some awful hour of trial, and have come out unsoiled and unscathed, there has been such a rapture in our souls. When we have stepped up to higher things on our dead selves, there has been such peace.

Do you know it? When you have accomplished something you did not think you could do; when you have made some sacrifice you thought you never could achieve; when you have done a noble thing—you have not thought about the nobility or loveliness of it, but there has been a delightful inner consciousness. One hardly knows what to call it. Bloom! The bloom of the flower! The light on the cloud! The hue of health on the face! The kiss of God! The ‘Well done, good and faithful servant!’ That is worth living for. This prize may be won here, and not yonder only. Every night after a day spent like this it seems as though God puts into our hearts, as we lie down upon our pillow to sleep, a jewel, which is part of our prize, and the accumulation of the jewels will make the felicity of Paradise.

20

THE ATTAINMENTS OF THE CHRISTIAN LIFE

Philippians 3:15,16

LET us therefore, as many as be perfect, be thus minded: and if in any thing ye be otherwise minded, God shall reveal even this unto you.

Nevertheless, whereto we have already attained, let us walk by the same rule, let us mind the same thing.

Phil. iii. 15, 16

THESE words suggest, that there is a great difference in the attainments of Christian people; and in endeavouring to bring this home, so that any who are laggard and sluggard may be quickened in the path of holiness, we may regard this chapter as falling naturally into a suite of some seven apartments, each of which leads to another, as in so many of the picturesque and princely homes of England. May God's Spirit help us to discover in which room we are already, and having discovered it, to press on to the next.

The Disrobing Room

'Circumcised the eighth day, of the stock of Israel, of the tribe of Benjamin, a Hebrew of Hebrews; as touching the law, a Pharisee; as touching zeal, persecuting the Church; as touching the righteousness which is in the law, found blameless. Howbeit what things were gain to me, these have I counted loss for Christ' (vv. 5-7). In the grey light of the dawn, we see the young Pharisee, decked out in all the paraphernalia of the dress of his order. His are the phylacteries, his the broad borders covered with texts, his the sacred cord as son of the law, over these the garment of zeal, and over this again a robe that seems spotless—'the righteousness of the law,' in which he accounts himself to be blameless. Around the room are burnished mirrors, and as he considers his array in the grey light he imagines himself to be highly commendable and likely to stand a good chance, not only in this world, but in the next. He can only think these things, because the light is so dim. Were it brighter, he would descry blemishes in his fairest robes. **Phil. iii. 15, 16**

The Two Pilgrims

Bunyan well describes such a man in his picture of Ignorance. You may remember how the two older pilgrims talked to the brisk youth as he walked beside them. They asked, 'How will you fare at the gate?'

'I shall fare as well as other people,' was the reply.

'What have you to show that will cause the gate to open, when you come to it?' they inquired.

'I know my Lord's will; I have been a good liver all my life; I pay every man his own; I pray constantly and fast; I pay and give alms; my heart is a good heart; I will never believe that it is as bad as you say.'

Bunyan's own Experience

In his *Grace Abounding* John Bunyan still further describes this condition :—

'Now,' he says after his outward amendment, 'I was become godly; now I was become a right honest man. Though as yet I was nothing but a poor

Phil. iii. 15, 16

painted hypocrite, yet I was proud of my godliness. I betook me to my Bible, and began to take great pleasure in reading, but especially with the historical part thereof; for as for Paul's Epistles, and such like Scriptures, I could not away with them, being as yet ignorant either of the corruptions of my nature or of the want and worth of Jesus Christ to save us.' 'The new birth did never enter into my mind; neither knew I the comfort of the word and promise, nor the deceitfulness and treachery of my own wicked heart. As for secret thoughts, I took no notice of them.'

Legal Righteousness laid aside

Whilst we stand gazing into this room, the grey light grows into the morning, and beneath its beams the young Pharisee, beholding himself in the mirrors around, flings off first the blameless robe of his legal righteousness, then strips off his zeal, then casts away his Pharisaic dress, puts aside his reliance upon the ordinances of Hebrewism. After stripping off one thing after another, as the revealing light shows how utterly sullied and blemished his robes are, he tramples them beneath his feet, and counts them as refuse and loss. He is horrified to think that if he had not known the light which came from the risen Lord, he might have gone forward to face the Great White Throne, and only then have discovered his mistake.

Have you entered this room? Have you stood beneath the light of God till you abhorred yourself? Have you come to see, with St Augustine, that the works in which you have been priding yourself are 'splendid sins?' Do you realise that, apart from the righteousness of Jesus Christ, your righteousness is as filthy rags? Oh, soul, thou wilt be as certainly lost as Ignorance was, who was carried to hell from the very gate of heaven, unless thou too standest in the revealing light of God, to show thee the insufficiency of anything and everything apart from a simple dependence upon the righteousness of His Son.

Phil. iii. 15, 16

The Robing Room

'And be found in Him, not having a righteousness of mine own, even that which is of the law, but that which is through faith in Christ, the righteousness which is of God by faith' (v. 9). 'One day,' says Bunyan, 'as I was passing into the field, and that too with some fear dashed on my conscience, fearing lest yet all was not right, suddenly, this sentence fell upon my soul, "Thy righteousness is in Heaven," and methought withal, I saw with the eyes of my soul, Jesus Christ at God's right hand: *there* was my righteousness; . . . I also saw, moreover, that it was not my good frame of heart that made my righteousness better, nor yet my bad frame of heart that made my righteousness worse; for my righteousness was Jesus Christ Himself, "The same yesterday, to-day, and for ever."'

In this, the robing room, the soul which had been stripped of all dependence upon itself, its frames, its feelings, its good desires, its alms, its prayers, its baptism, its conversion, its church membership,—and having put all these beneath its feet, receives from the hand of God a perfected righteousness, the righteousness which is from God by faith, a robe which the fingers of Christ have woven, a justification

Phil. iii. 15, 16

which His blood has purchased, and which His hand bestows to the open hand of faith.

Hast thou realised this? Hast thou attained unto this? Art thou standing arrayed in this?—for in death, and judgment, and eternity, nothing will avail thee but to be clothed in the perfect spotless righteousness of Christ, who was made sin for us, though He knew no sin, that we might be made the Righteousness of God in Him.

The Room of Intimate Fellowship with Jesus

'That I may know Him, and the power of His resurrection, and the fellowship of His sufferings, becoming conformed unto His death' (v. 10). As we look into that chamber, we find that hard by the entrance is a deep grave-like aperture. It looks as though a tomb had been hollowed out in the stone floor; beyond is a table on which the bread and wine commemorate the body and blood of Christ; against the wall a rough and heavy cross is planted; affixed to the wall are a scourge, and a crown of thorns. The room, therefore, might seem forbidding, were it not that a celestial light shines full upon the thorn-crown, and whilst we look, it seems as though it were gleaming with jewels, as though the topaz, jasper, carbuncle, and all manner of precious stones had been caught amid the thorns, and become woven into its texture. Every day the true-hearted soul must enter that room. We must never really get beyond it in this life. It must constantly be our resort, that we may know Christ and the power of His Resurrection.

The order of this verse appears to stand in the reverse direction to our experience. It begins with knowing Him; then it passes to the power of His

Phil. iii. 15, 16

Conformable to the Lord's Death

resurrection, then to the fellowship of His sufferings, and lastly, to conformableness with His death. With many, the reverse is the way by which they are led. That is, they begin by being 'conformable to His death.' Do you know what it is to lie down in that grave of Christ, till the voices of the world's tumult and the throb of passion subside, till you realise how little this world is, and how much eternity? Have you attained to this? Have you become conformed unto His death? What was that death? In its judicial aspect, an atonement for human sin; but looking at it from the human and personal side it was the bringing of every natural desire into absolute subjection to the Will and Law of God—the desire to live, the desire for love, the desire for popular adulation, and human friendship. From the earliest of His recorded temptations, our Lord made this the rule of His Life. He would not gratify the natural appetite of hunger until He was certain of being in the line of His Father's Will. This is what the Cross means, and this involved Calvary. If, then, our Master would not make stones of the desert bread, to feed His natural hunger, because the Father had not bade Him eat, we may not yield, even to what seems natural, until our Father says we may. And if we carry out that principle of subordinating everything to the will of the Father, we shall certainly come to the Cross, and out of the Cross comes the diadem of victory. You conform to His death, you eat of His flesh, you drink of His blood, and then pass on to know the power of His resurrection.

Phil. iii. 15, 16

But as we have seen, the reverse is also true, and happy are they who have experienced it. They begin by knowing Jesus in the most intimate and blessed fellowship, and almost without realising it they are led on to realise that they are walking with Him, not in the energy of their own nature, but in the powers of His Resurrection. The Spirit of Holiness, who raised their Lord from the dead, is doing the same for them, they experience the mighty energies that emanate from the risen Saviour, and in His strength walk on their high places. But in doing so, they are brought in contact with the virulent hatred of their fellows. As men hated the Master of the House, they hate those of His household. The full tide of human opposition surges up against them, as an adverse current which breaks in clouds of spray on the undaunted progress of an ocean steamer. Presently the beast that ascendeth out of the bottomless abyss makes war against them, and overcomes and kills them, and their dead bodies lie in the street of the great city, which spiritually is called Sodom and Egypt, where also their Lord was crucified; but after three days and an half the Spirit of Life from God enters into them, and they stand upon their feet, and they hear a great voice from heaven saying unto them, 'Come up hither.' (See Rev. xi. 6-12.) They know the fellowship of Christ's sufferings, and are made conformable unto His death, but they attain to His Resurrection. They drink of His cup, and are baptised with His Baptism, and so come to sit on His Throne.

The Room of High Endeavour

'Brethren, I count not myself yet to have apprehended; but one thing I do, forgetting the things which are behind, and stretching forward to the things which are before, I press on toward the goal, unto the prize of the high calling of God in Christ Jesus' (vv. 13, 14). In this room are various pictures of Alpine ascents, photographs of the high summits which other souls have scaled. Around are the prizes that have been won in the arena by successful conflict. On every side are the marks of achievement; and in the midst of the room, unfurled as though it were soon to be grasped and borne forth, is a banner with the 'strange device,' *Excelsior*! Everything, therefore, that betokens past achievement is accounted but as the stepping-stone to still further effort. The soul leaves behind it as a mere memory, the things which it has attained, however great and beautiful in themselves, because some higher ascent calls to it. Is this the attitude of your soul? **Phil. iii. 15, 16**

Have you forgotten some things?

Have you learnt to forget? Are you living upon your past attempts, their failure, or success, for any of these will cut the sinews of your strength? You must forget even your sins, God forgets them, saying, Try again. You must forget your innocence, the innocence of your childhood; purity tried by fire is better. You must forget, also, your realised ideals. You must forget things which have become dear to you, but which have hindered you, clinging to you as barnacles to the bottom of the great steamer, hindering its progress. You must forget all that, and from this day must confess that you have not attained, that you are not perfected, but are going to climb to the rare heights of Christ-likeness; always doing

Phil. iii. 15, 16

what Christ would do, if He were in your place; always taking as the sufficient question of your life, 'What would Jesus do if He were situated as I am?'

The Room of Compassion

'Many walk, of whom I told you often, and now tell you even weeping, that they are the enemies of the Cross of Christ; whose end is perdition, whose god is their belly, and whose glory is in their shame' (vv. 18, 19). There is a tear bottle here, in which the tears of Christ were caught once, though long since they have been transmuted into the pearls that glisten in His crown. But that tear bottle is there for the tears of those disciples who have learnt His compassion; for as the Redeemer wept, so do His redeemed weep still, and say, even weeping, of others, 'They are the enemies of the Cross of Christ.' May that compassion, like a fountain, send the tears in rills from our eyes. God forbid that we should live in such a world as this, without weeping over the enemies of the Cross; and it should be borne in mind that the enemies of the Cross, here referred to, are not those who have rejected Christ, but those who once professed Christianity, and had the creed and reputation of godliness, but in their heart of hearts, and in their lives, have denied the Lord that bought them.

The Room of Expectant Hope

'Our citizenship is in Heaven; from whence also we wait for a Saviour, the Lord Jesus Christ' (v. 20). This room has a window looking East; and it is so situated that it is hardly possible to descry the river; for the view lies across the river, to a fair and beautiful horizon; and the soul which has passed through the earlier stages, stands with eye fixed, and every nerve and muscle strained, looking for the dawn, whilst the morning star shines clear in the sky. 'We look for a Saviour.' It is the saved soul that waits for the Saviour. We are saved from the wrath of God; we are being saved day by day from the power of sin; but, oh, we long for Him who shall appear the second time, without sin, unto salvation!

The Room of Confident Anticipation

'Who shall fashion anew the body of our humiliation, that it may be conformed to the body of His glory, according to the working whereby He is able even to subject all things unto Himself' (v. 21). *To subject.* Look at this. He who, in the second chapter was subjected, in this chapter subjects. You must be subjected before you can subject.

(1) We confidently anticipate the moment when the body of our humiliation, which has so often limited and hindered us in our work, which has hungered and thirsted, fainted and grown weary, whose eyes have failed, whose knees have faltered, and hands hung down, shall exchange its corruption for incorruption, its mortality for immortality, being transfigured into the likeness of the body of His glory—ethereal, vigorous, incapable of fatigue but a perfected instrument for a perfected nature.

(2) We anticipate much more than that. Death, thou shalt be subdued. Grave, thou shalt be subdued. Sin, sorrow, pain, evil, ye shall be subdued. The Lord comes to subdue you as we confidently expect. This room enshrines masterpieces of art, commemorating the great past. That picture is of the overthrow of Pharaoh; and that of the destruc-

Phil. iii. 15, 16 tion of Midian; and that of the defeat of those mighty Assyrian hosts which menaced Hezekiah; and here are the cross and empty grave—symbols of the victory of the Son of God over the world, the flesh, and the devil. Yes! He *shall* overcome; it is His right. He shall subject all things unto Himself; it is the Father's promise. The kingdoms of this world shall become the kingdoms of our God, and of His Christ, and He shall reign for ever. Let us hasten unto the coming of that day of God!

21

BURGESSES OF HEAVEN

Philippians 3:17-21

BRETHREN, be followers together of me, and mark them which walk so as ye have us for an ensample.

(For many walk, of whom I have told you often, and now tell you even weeping, *that they are* the enemies of the cross of Christ:

Whose end *is* destruction, whose God *is their* belly, and *whose* glory *is* in their shame, who mind earthly things.)

For our conversation is in heaven; from whence also we look for the Saviour, the Lord Jesus Christ:

Who shall change our vile body, that it may be fashioned like unto His glorious body, according to the working whereby He is able even to subdue all things unto Himself.

Phil. iii. 17-21

THE Greek word translated *conversation* is, as we saw in i. 27, the root from which we derive our word politics, politician, policeman, and such like; and the true rendering in each case should be *citizenship.* In the earlier passage it might be rendered: 'Be true citizens of God's commonwealth—let your life befit your high calling to be burgesses of the New Jerusalem'; and in this passage it might be rendered: 'Your city home is in heaven.'

The same thought pervades the Scriptures. 'Now they desire a better country, that is, a heavenly' (Heb. xi. 16). 'The city which hath foundations, whose builder and maker is God' (v. 10). Even the patriarchs descried and greeted from afar the palaces of that heavenly city. And the inspired writer takes up the same attitude when he says: 'Here we have no continuing city, but we seek one to come.'

Phil. iii.
17-21

Our Citizenship in Heaven

* * *

If we would resemble the saints of past days we must conceive of our citizenship as being in Heaven. That a man should be a citizen of a city, but live in a foreign country, is not an unusual circumstance. In these days when men are scattered so widely over the world, many of the citizens of London are to be found in India, Burmah, and Australia, on a visit for temporary purposes; and so the anomaly is often presented of men being strangers in the place where they are resident, but most at home in the city from which they are absent.

What is true of the pilgrim-life was pre-eminently true of Jesus Christ, who said of Himself, 'He that came down from heaven, the Son of Man who is in heaven,' as though during His earthly life He recognised that His citizenship in His Father's city remained unimpaired, and that residence for thirty years amongst men did not naturalise Him as a citizen of earth.

In the collect for Advent Sunday we are told that the Son of God came to *visit* us in great humility; and four times over in the Gospels the Lord's life on earth is described as a visit. All the time He was amongst men, He was a citizen of that city, therefore He lay in a borrowed manger; His body was deposited in a borrowed grave; He had not where to lay His head; and when every man went to his own home, He went to the Mount of Olives. Throughout His life He was a pilgrim and foreigner as all the fathers were.

Like Master, like Man

And what is true of Jesus Christ should be true of every Christian. As Lady Powerscourt puts it: 'The

Christian is not a man who, standing on earth, looks up to heaven; but who, being in heaven, looks down upon earth, and throughout his life he recognises that he is a foreigner indeed.' And this very aspect of the Christian will bring him into conflict with the men of this world, for when he says in his Master's words: 'I am not of this world, I am from above, ye are from beneath,' they gnash their teeth at him, and cast him out, as the citizens of Vanity Fair did Christian and his companion. One of the Puritans sweetly says: 'It cannot be expected that the men of this world can ever understand the Christian life, because they have never been in the City from which he hails, and therefore are altogether ignorant of its manner of life and mode of speech.' The world is unable to recognise us, because our language, speech, dress, manner, and method of life are altogether different from that which is in vogue in its society. If unconverted men lay their hands upon your shoulders to hail you as one of themselves, begin to question in your own heart whether you are truly living as one of the citizens of the New Jerusalem.

Phil. iii. 17-21

* * *

This Citizenship is a Matter of Birthright

In a memorable moment, when the Apostle had been delivered from his foes, he asserted his right to be interrogated without scourging, on the ground of his being a Roman citizen. The chief captain was immediately informed and hastened to his side. 'A Roman? With great price I obtained this right!' 'Ah!' the Apostle said, 'but I was freeborn, my birth carried with it the right of citizenship.' Yes, and the residence of a thousand years in Heaven

Phil. iii. 17-21

would not make us more certainly citizens of the New Jerusalem, than we are at this moment, if we are born from above. Grant that we still live on this side of the veil which hides the transient from the enduring, the temporal from the eternal, the seen from the unseen, yet, so soon as we are regenerate of the Holy Spirit, in the first moment of our new life, we become enrolled in the list of burgesses, we have the franchise of the New Jerusalem given to us, our names are entered upon its directory. Though as yet we have not taken up the right, and entered into the enjoyment of all that awaits us, we have, nevertheless, the right to enter in through the gate into the city. This may not help you much now, but, I pray you, meditate on it for a few moments daily, and you will find it becoming a growing force to withdraw you from the things of this world, and to attach you to the things of the other world; you will come to reckon that you must set your affection on that city to which you belong, that you must lay up your treasures there where neither moth nor rust corrupt, and that you must regulate your conduct by the regulations that rule in that city. Every regenerate person, by the fact of the new birth, has obtained the franchise of the City of God.

* * *

To belong to that City should be a Matter of Joy and Pride

Athens was the glory of Greece, and though the smaller states and cities were in perpetual conflict, every Greek was proud of her peerless beauty and culture. The citizen of Rome, travelling afar, bore himself as a stronger, prouder man, because he could say, 'I am a Roman.' And if we could really see things as they are, and disentangle ourselves from the net of the material, there is nothing of which we should be more proud, than to belong to that great commonwealth which includes all pure and holy souls of every age, and which shall stand when all cities and politics, all thrones and empires have disappeared, as the foam on the wave that bears it. Phil. iii. 17-21

Men speak of Rome as the eternal city. She has no right to that title. There is only one eternal city, because its foundations cannot be impaired by revolution or change; because its walls are founded on God's eternal covenant of truth; and because all its laws and regulations are based upon the principles of eternal truth. From out of those city gates proceed the angels to all parts of the universe, but they return to it, as the metropolis of life. Thither the kings and princes of science, of literature, of music, of art bring their treasures. The saints of every age find their home there. Her light is brighter than the sun's; there is no temple because God is her Temple; her river is the Holy Spirit of God; her flowers are of amaranth; her streets are of gold; her walls of jasper; her gates of pearl; God Himself is her architect and King. Who may not be rightly proud to belong to such a city! The Goths who conquered the Roman Empire for God broke upon it like an avalanche from another world; and because they were so utterly indifferent to its attractions, they were easily able to overcome it. Who can overcome the world, but those who have our faith—the faith which detaches from this world, because it attaches us to the unseen and eternal, in

Phil. iii. 17-21

God and His Christ? The Church of God will never be able to conquer the world so long as she is part of it, but only as she comes on the world from the sphere above it, with the impulse and impetus of those who believe that their city lies beyond the stars.

* * *

We are to walk worthy of it

The Apostle says that there were men in that time who professed the Cross, but who were 'enemies of the Cross.' Neither Paine nor Voltaire ever inflicted such awful havoc on the religion of Jesus Christ as those false professors who have borne His name, but been destitute of His grace and power. Such men, the Apostle says, *mind earthly things.* They were made to face God like kings, but they are always rooting in the earth like swine; their ambitions are limited by the horizon of time and sense. They glory in things of which they ought to be ashamed; appetite is their God, and destruction their end.

A story is told of a man of wealth who was taking his friend round his magnificent mansion, in which a spacious chamber was dedicated to be a chapel. The visitor, who thought of little else than good living, on entering the chapel, said: 'What a magnificent kitchen this would make.' Whereupon his host replied: 'You are mistaken, this is not a kitchen; when I have made my belly my God, then I will make my chapel my kitchen, but not before.' How many men there are whose one thought is set on eating and drinking, and the gratification of sensual appetite. There is no chapel in their life, it is all kitchen.

Burgesses of Heaven

* * *

Phil. iii. 17-21

We must keep an Eye upon the City Gates

That word *whence*, by the peculiar construction of the Greek, does not refer to the heavens, but to the city gate. It is a very tender and fragrant thought that whilst transacting our business on the lowlands of earth, we may ever keep our eye on the city gate into which He entered, whom we love, and through which He will most certainly come again as a Saviour. 'Whence, also, we look for the Saviour,' 'He shall come the second time without sin unto salvation.' In these dark and dreadful days the Church needs to turn with unceasing hope towards the Second Advent. Oh! when will those pearly gates open! When will that cavalcade issue forth! When through the dim haze will the Lord come, riding upon His white horse, and followed by the army of Heaven. Come quickly, come quickly, O Saviour of men, Who by Thy first coming didst put away our sin, and by Thy second coming will put the crown on the work of salvation by raising and changing our mortal body!

Our Vile Body

In the old version we read *our vile body*. When Archbishop Whately was dying, he asked his chaplain to read to him. The chaplain took up this paragraph reading it as it stands in the A.V. 'Stop,' said the Archbishop, 'not "vile body," if you please, but body of our humiliation.' The body is not *vile* in the ordinary significance of the word, because Jesus bore it, because His blood purchased it, because the Spirit makes it His Temple, and because it has been so often the medium by which holy impressions have gone forth

Phil. iii. 17-21

to others. Not vile; but the body of our humiliation, because it cramps, confines, and limits us; it needs sleep and food; it retains in its very organism the impression of past sins; it is a clanking chain, that holds us down when we would fain rise, so that one understands something of what chained eagles feel, when they fret against the iron bars of their cage, and pine to soar on outspread pinions to the sun.

'The body of our humiliation,' but it shall be transfigured. It shall rise from its dust, and shall be changed in a moment, in the twinkling of an eye, into the likeness of 'the body of His glory.' We stand upon the transfiguration mount, and behold the body of His glory. We wait with Mary at the open grave, and see the body of His glory. Finally, from the Ascension Mount, we follow the body of His glory, and behold it, shining as the sun. It seems impossible to believe that one day we shall be like Him, and that our mortal shall be radiant with immortality like His.

How shall it be?

How shall these things be? There is but one answer. 'By the working whereby he is able to subdue all things unto Himself.' Say this over and over again. When the devil is strong, when passion rages, when you cannot be the man you would, when it seems as though the world were hopelessly corrupt and the wrongs of time refuse to be adjusted, repeat these words to yourself, as a sweet refrain: 'The power by which He is able to subdue all things unto Himself.' Oh, take to Thyself Thy great power and reign! Begin now with obdurate wills, with proud and evil hearts, with indomitable pride, with passion and lust. Subdue these, O Christ, and cause us to be transfigured in the spirit, that whilst in the body of humiliation, we may live worthily of our citizenship, and ultimately rise to the life immortal. Phil. iii. 17-21

The Joy of the Coming

It is said that as the cattle, which may have been greatly demoralised by the tossing of the vessel and the discomfort of their quarters, draw near land, at the end of a tedious voyage, and scent the breeze, which comes over the ship laden with the fragrance of the clover, the effect is immediate, they begin to revive, and toss their heads as though they were keenly conscious that the voyage was almost over, and that the familiar pasture-lands were within reach. So should we look with reviving hope for the coming of Christ, who will put down all rule and authority and power, will subdue all things to Himself, and complete our salvation which begins with the forgiveness and deliverance from the curse, which proceeds to the ever deepening emancipation from the power of corruption, and which will end when this body of humiliation is delivered from the last remains and traces of the fall, and raised in the perfect beauty of the everlasting morning.

Is it wonderful that in the first verse of the following chapter, the Apostle turns to the Philippians as his 'beloved and longed for brethren,' and bids them stand fast? The vision and hope of future glory, when these mortal bodies shall be conformed to the Body of the glory of our Risen Lord, and when the privileges of our heavenly citizenship shall

Phil. iii. 17-21 be fully realised, were surely enough to hold them steady as the anchor holds the ship. By all the promises that had been made to them, by all the hopes they cherished, by all the glory which was already flushing the horizon, he urged them to stand fast in the Lord, watching that they should not lose their reward, and waiting until the fulness of the times should bring in the fulness of their redemption.

22

'THE LORD IS AT HAND.'

Philippians 4:1-6

THEREFORE, my brethren, dearly beloved and longed for, my joy and crown, so stand fast in the Lord, *my* dearly beloved.

I beseech Euodias, and beseech Syntyche, that they be of the same mind in the Lord.

And I intreat thee also, true yokefellow, help those women which laboured with me in the gospel, with Clement also, and *with* other my fellow-labourers, whose names *are* in the book of life.

Rejoice in the Lord alway: *and* again I say, Rejoice.

Let your moderation be known unto all men. The Lord *is* at hand.

Be careful for nothing; but in every thing by prayer and supplication with thanksgiving let your requests be made known unto God.

Phil. iv. 1-6

Paul and the Lord's Advent

THAT has generally been thought to indicate the Apostle's belief in the Lord's imminent advent, which, as we know, was a prevalent motive with the early Church. If a missionary left his native land, and crossed the ocean with the Evangel, as the burnished mirror of the water shone with the path of the sunbeams, it seemed to him that at any moment, down those sunbeams, the Lord might come. When the primitive Christian said good-bye to his fellow-Christian, it was without too great a pang of regret, because they expected soon to meet in the presence of Christ. Every tremor in the air, every catastrophe, every political change appeared to them like the first

Phil. iv. 1-6

note of the archangel's trumpet, like the footfall of the coming Prince. This consciousness of the imminent advent was a mighty lever, by which to lift the whole state of thought and feeling in the early Church to those higher levels, the best and most glorious levels, which the Church of God has ever attained.

But for one or two reasons such does not appear to be the meaning here. First, the Greek word does not lend itself to that significance. The better rendering undoubtedly would be 'the Lord is near.' Secondly, at the end of the third chapter, the Apostle had been dilating upon the expectant attitude in which we wait for the Saviour, and it would be hardly compatible with that to find him immediately saying, The Lord is here. Thirdly, it is interesting to notice that the Apostle's anticipation of the advent of Christ was, as the years passed, largely affected by his growing conception of the nearness of Christ, so that all life was to be lived 'in Him.' He never gave up his hope of the advent, but he became gloriously influenced by the larger thought that all life must be ensphered in Christ.

Whilst inditing this paragraph he became suddenly overshadowed with the consciousness that the Lord

The Lord ever near

Jesus Christ was literally present in his hired room, nearer to him than the sentry, nearer to him than Epaphroditus, nearer to him than Timothy, his beloved son, and he burst out with this exclamation, which his amanuensis at once wove into the fabric of the Epistle: 'The Lord is near; He is with me in my room, and He is with you in Philippi; and we are all included and encircled in the golden fence of His presence.' Phil. iv. 1-6

There is a similar instance of this in Ps. cxix., where the holy author stays in the midst of the royal sweep of his work, and cries: 'Thou art near, O God.' We all know times like that. We have been walking in the midst of some beautiful landscape, the river rushing past, flowers dipping their cups silently into its brink, the gentle air moving through the quivering leaves above, the insect life humming its varied music, and all nature suffused with the smile of the sun. Then, all suddenly, there has been borne in on us the consciousness of a spiritual presence; we have felt a breath on our faces, a thrill in our hearts, and, behold, He who came to John on the Isle of Patmos has come to us; and, lo, the radiant glory of Christ has excelled that of the sun. 'Thou art near, O God; the Lord is near.'

To everyone of us

In the church, when saying your prayers mechanically, falling in with the murmur of repetition as you have done a thousand times, standing listlessly listening to the people singing, or joining with them without much heart; sitting apparently intent on the words of the minister whilst your thoughts have been far away on your business or pleasure, suddenly there has been as it were the music of golden bells, and you have realised that the old promise was being fulfilled: 'There am I in the midst.' Without opening the door, without the sound of a footfall, the Lord Jesus has glided into the shut apartment of your nature, and you have said, 'The Lord is near.'

The Power of Presence

What a mighty power a presence is to some of

us! To a man, the presence of a pure and noble woman has often put a cool hand upon a fevered forehead, stayed the throb of passion, and called him back to sanity and manhood. And to a woman how much there is in the presence of her husband, lover, brother, or friend! How strong and calm she becomes when she is made conscious of that presence! With some of us there is the radiant vision given by memory of a beloved parent, of the sainted minister of our childhood, or of the servant of God whose fragrant biography we have read. How many of us have been calmed, quieted, and restrained by the presence through memory and recollection of someone whom we have loved and lost! How pathetic it was when our late beloved Queen in dying called thrice, 'Albert, Albert, Albert!' How certainly those words revealed the presence in which she had lived! Probably there are many men and women whose lives are lived in the consciousness of the presence of the Angel of their Pilgrimage. How often we have been restrained from things we are glad we never did, and words we are thankful we never said, by the thought that the angels were at hand, and we knew that they would blush, that their holy natures would be hurt, unless we were strong, gentle, and pure.

But, oh! if every one of us would live, not in the presence of the beloved wife or noble woman; of the strong, brave husband; of the holy memory, or of the peerless angel, but in the presence of the Lord Jesus, saying perpetually to ourselves, 'The Lord is near, the Lord is at hand,' there is not one of us that would not spring up into an altogether new life, as flowers do when from the arctic they are removed to the tropic soil, and instead of being environed by frost become the nurslings of the sunny air. If every one of us could do as the late Mr Spurgeon did, who said that he did not recollect spending a quarter of an hour without the distinct thought of the presence of Christ, life would become ever so much better, brighter, and stronger than it is. **Phil. iv. 1-6**

The Presence of Christ

The presence of Jesus Christ is brought home to us by the Holy Ghost, who is the Spirit of Remembrance, making Him real, recalling our wandering thoughts, and concentrating them on Him until He stands out luminous and kingly in our life. That is Christianity. With too many the Christian religion consists in living back in the past. They linger in Gethsemane rather than in Joseph's garden, with its empty grave. This is the life of the Roman Catholic, or of those who have been nursed in Protestant schools of thought, but have never learnt the meaning of the Lord's Ascension. But true Christianity does not postpone the presence of Christ to the future, or recall it from the past, but lives in the sense that *He is.* Hence the Gospel by St John contains such recurring phrases as: I am the Vine; I am the Good Shepherd; I am the Door; I am the Resurrection and the Life. Christ lives in the present tense, and blessed is the soul that has learnt that lesson.

The whole of this paragraph (verses 1-7) *crystallises around this thought.*

Steadfastness

Verse 1: *Steadfastness.* The man who is backwards and forwards, mercurial, easily up to boiling

Phil. iv. 1-6

point, and as soon down to zero, who is on the hooks and off ten times a week, now like a seraph flashing with zeal, now like a snail crawling in lethargy, who is everything by fits and starts and nothing long, will not have a happy Christian experience, nor will his influence tell in the Church or on the world. He may be a genius, but he will be a meteor dying in the dark. It is better to have for a friend and fellow-worker a man of less brilliance and with fewer ideas, who will be occupied by one thought, and give it regular and patient expression. In life, as in war, it is not the man that makes brilliant dashes, but he who can pursue a plan of strategy, week after week, that succeeds.

In the Lord

The source of stability is to stand fast *in the Lord.* Our only hope of stability is in union with 'the Rock.'

There is a sculpture in Spain of the Crucifixion, which is the only one of the kind. A fierce light falls on it from a hidden window. One hand is nailed to the Cross, the other is stretched out. The story is that lovers plighted their troth there, and afterwards, when the man was faithless, the woman came back to plead her case beneath the Cross, and the hand disengaged itself, and stretched towards her, whilst a voice said : 'I was witness.' Probably, however, the old sculptor meant that if one hand is nailed to the Cross in atonement, the other hand is quick to help ; and if you want help to be stable, you will find a very present help in the thought that He is near.

Like-minded-ness

Verses 2, 3 : *Be of the same mind.* These two

women, Euodia and Syntyche, had fallen out; two women of whom the Apostle says: 'They laboured with me in the Gospel,' and the Greek word is—*they agonised by my side.* What a tribute to women! All through the centuries they have wrought beside their ministers. Compute what the churches owe to women. Many of them must have been disbanded if holy women had not bound them together by their presence and their prayer. Think of all the children like Chrysostom—'golden-mouthed'—who have been reared by Christian mothers; of all the hymns in our hymn-books we owe to women. But Euodia and Syntyche had fallen out. They were of different dispositions, and could not understand each other. They had been made on a different plan. Paul knew that neither Clement nor his fellow-labourers could put them right, but that if those two women came into the presence of Jesus they would find it easy to be of one mind. In the presence of the sun hard icicles flow together.

Phil. iv. 1-6

Rejoicing

Verse 4: *Rejoice always.* When your children are around you, and when *crêpe* is on your knocker; when your books show a good profit on the year's trading, and when your best schemes have miscarried; 'Rejoice *always.*' Amid your tears keep a trustful, restful, joyful heart, not rejoicing in your gifts, in your successes, in your friends, but in Him—rejoice in the Lord, in the presence of the Lord, for He is always there. The secret of perennial joy is in the realised companionship of the Redeemer.

Forbearance

Verse 5: *Moderation.* The Revised Version says *forbearance.* We should say in modern English

Phil. iv. 1-6

sweet reasonableness. Luther, in his translation, renders it *yieldingness.* Of course, we can never yield principle ; we can never yield to men who are doing the devil's work in the world ; but a good many have edges and corners which concern temperament rather than principle, and we who know them ought to yield, just as the boat in descending a very narrow streamlet has to take the course of the stream. It is easy to bear all, to endure all, to believe all, when the overshadowing presence of the Lord Jesus is realised.

Garrisoned in Christ

Verse 7 : *The peace of God, which passeth all understanding, shall guard your hearts and your thoughts in Christ Jesus.* It is only in the presence of Christ that this peace becomes ours.

Worried and anxious with the fluctuation of stock and share markets, his employés and subordinates trying him ; the master unreasonable ; affairs in a tangle ; a man comes home from his day's work feeling thoroughly out of heart. His wife meets him at the door, her face calm and restful ; there is a sense of peace and serenity, like the scent of flowers, in the room where she had been awaiting him. She knows that the frost has gathered about him, as the frost gathered on the *Majestic* one winter day when it came into New York harbour, after battling with the Atlantic. She ministers to his needs, and presently elicits, without seeming to do it, the story of the day. Without realising the change which is transpiring, he pours his confidences into her ear, and as he does so, the thaw sets in, his heart softens, and by-and by it seems as though the white-robed Angel of Peace passes from her heart to his to keep its affections and thoughts. We all know something like that; and that is the idea of the Apostle, to live in the presence of Jesus, and to turn to Him from every anxiety and worry, so as to allow His presence to saturate and soothe the soul. Phil. iv. 1-6

The Lord is at hand. Say it when you need to be stable. Say it when Euodia has quarrelled with Syntyche. Say it when your joy threatens to fail. Say it when you are irritated and think there is no reason you should yield so persistently to another. Say it when you are worried and anxious. Until you come into that presence many things will seem impossible, which beneath the light of those deep tender eyes will become easy as newly mown lawns to tired feet.

Are you one to whom the presence of Jesus is dreadful? Then Heaven can be no place for you, where He is Lord. Bring your strong will to Him; ask Him to break or bend it; give yourself to Him, and ask the Holy Spirit that from this moment, in temptation, in sin, when torn with conviction, when smarting with pain, in perplexity, in death, and in judgment, the one thought of your life may be that the Lord is at hand.

23

THE SENTINEL OF THE HEART

Philippians 4:7

AND the peace of God, which passeth all understanding, shall keep your hearts and minds through Christ Jesus.

Phil iv. 7

The Apostles' Campaign

IN the course of our Lord's instructions to His Apostles, in which He appointed their route, and gave them their commission, He did not hesitate to tell them of the unfriendly reception with which the world would receive their ministry. They would be as sheep amid wolves; would be delivered up to councils, and scourged in synagogues; would be brought before governors and kings; would be hated of all men for His name's sake; would be driven from city to city; would be called upon to lay down their lives—very rough and unfriendly would be the response of men to the ministry that meant only good.

Conditions of Warfare

He did not hesitate also to strip them of all needless encumbrance. They were to carry no purse and no money; they were not to provide a scrip in which to place the victuals that kindly hands might offer them; they were to be content with one coat, not even reserving a second against wear and tear or inclement weather; they were to refuse the heavy boots shod with metal which the Roman soldiers had introduced into the country, and to be content with simple sandals; they were to be satisfied with the pilgrim's staff, if they happened to possess it—otherwise they were not to endeavour to procure one; they were to start out in fellowship with God, whose workmen they were, sure that He would at least supply them with food. Like the soldiers of whom the Apostle speaks, they were not to encumber themselves with baggage. Their movements were to be unimpeded, their hearts free from all anxious thought and care, their faith in perpetual exercise in Him who had called them to work in His great harvest field. **Phil. iv. 7**

Welcome or Unwelcome

On arriving at any new town or village, the Gospel messengers were to ask of the first group they met the names and residences of any who were known throughout the place as generous and well-disposed; to such they were to make application for hospitality during their brief sojourn in the place. On reaching the threshold of the house, they were to utter, with something more than a formal greeting, the Eastern benediction, 'Peace be to this house.' They were then to wait, carefully noting the result.

It might be that no 'son of peace' would be found within the doors; no calm, quiet face would welcome them with a smile; no heart at leisure from itself would be able to answer them back with words of peace; but instead, there would be the scowl, the cold and formal manner, the evident antipathy.

Welcomed where 'A Son of Peace' was

On the other hand, the 'son of peace' might be discovered within that household—the householder

Phil. iv. 7 himself, or his wife, or little child, or someone more obscure amongst the servants. There would be an instant welcome from that soul, which was in living affinity with the greeting of peace; and this would at once indicate that such a house was the predestined home in which the heralds of the Gospel of Peace should stay, eating and drinking such things as were set before them, until they departed to fulfil their commission elsewhere. How simple, primitive, and beautiful the whole arrangement was, and how Oriental!

The meeting between the Apostles, commissioned to bear with them the peace of Christ, and the 'son of peace,' fulfilling in some Hebrew home an obscure life, on whom the benediction of a larger peace than he had ever known would henceforth rest, suggests that there are two kinds of peace in the world—that of Christ and that of man, that which comes from above and that which is elaborated through the process of human thought and prudence, the one that passes understanding and the other that is within the limits of understanding. It may be, that from this moment, the peace that passeth understanding shall come in to abide in hearts which up till now have been content with something less than God's best. It may be, that some will understand, as never before, what Jesus meant when He said: '*My peace* I give unto you; not as the world giveth, give I unto you. Let not your heart be troubled.' Who is there that does not long for *His* peace? Who does not desire to have something better than the peace with which the world contents itself?

In many a Jewish home this type of character could be found;—men who owned their vineyard, or gathered the berries of their olives, enjoyed the comfort of their modest patrimony, were happily married, and rejoiced in the filial affection of their children. They supported the local synagogue, stood well with their neighbours and friends, gave generously to the poor, and did not fail to attend the great annual feasts at Jerusalem. Their life flowed through the years easily and pleasantly, like a river gliding between its banks in the verdant plains—such men might be called 'sons of peace.' Their houses would be open to the entertainment of strangers; their manner would be suave and pleasant; there would be no grudging on their table, no stinting of their gifts; they would have no foes, but would bask in the sunshine of universal favour. Like Job, such men would look forward to dying in their nest, to passing from the town or village where they had spent their happy days to rest in Abraham's bosom. Surely, however, the peace of such characters is not of the highest type. The comfort and prosperity of their lives are largely dependent on the substantial buildings and ample provision which they have made for themselves.

Phil. iv. 7

The Peace that can be understood

Are there not many men of to-day like these? They are comfortably provided for, have a balance at their bankers', are possessed of good health and good spirits, are happily wedded, the parents of noble children, and surrounded by everything that can promote the well-being and prosperity of life; and surely the conditions and foundations of such peace

Modern Parallels

Phil. iv. 7

are well within the limits of anyone's understanding. They look round their lives to see any possible source of trouble or annoyance that may be menacing them, and having discovered it, they do their best to provide against it. They go round the house of their life to see how far it is secure against tempests and flood, and wherever they discover a weak spot they use their best endeavour to strengthen it, and having done all, they retire to the interior and rest in peace, in fancied security against whatever storm may arise.

Some Grounds of Peace

The peace of one man arises from the fact that he has managed to secure a competence, or to accumulate a little balance in the bank; his peace of mind, as he looks forward upon old age, is due to the fact that there is something to secure him against want. Another accounts himself safe because he is allied with rich friends, or enjoys good health, or is held in high social esteem, and he comforts himself in view of any contingency by saying: 'My friends will help me through; the momentum of my life will carry me over these rapids; I have done so much for others, surely they will stand by me when my evil day arrives.' Yet another finds his peace in some system of thought which he has elaborated, and in virtue of which he holds himself ready to answer any puzzling question that may be addressed to him. Whatever controversy may be hurtling through the world, he feels it cannot come near him, so carefully has he wrought out his system as a wall of defence.

But Uncertain Grounds

All these men are 'sons of peace.' They have

peace which can be easily understood. They are not in trouble as other men, not plagued as other men; from year to year the stream of their life flows evenly forward. They have homes, incomes, abounding vigour, high spirits, happy family relations, and perhaps some faith in God as their Father and Redeemer; but it is easy to see the foundations upon which the superstructure of their peace rests. It is very pleasant and innocent, but there is always a serious liability of its being disturbed. As someone suggests, it reminds one of Robinson Crusoe when he first landed upon his island. He built his hut, reared his stockade, planted his cornfield, penned in his goats, primed his gun, but he knew nothing of the land that lay beyond the thin fringe of trees which skirted the shore, and at any moment, from the unknown territory beyond, a horde of cannibals, or herds of wild beasts, might sweep down upon the spot which he had selected for his home. His peace was limited, and was always liable to be suddenly broken. It is not enough for us to have the peace which arises from earthly conditions, and the possession of good things. There is a deeper, sweeter peace, which the Apostle describes as passing all understanding; and our Lord refers to it when He says: 'My peace I give, not as the world giveth.' Phil. iv. 7

The Peace which passes Understanding

This was the peace of Christ and His Apostles. There was nothing to account for it. Not theirs the settled home; not theirs the wife and child; not theirs the provision against the future; not theirs a universal love and welcome; not theirs the prospect of a serene old age, surrounded by troops of friends.

Phil. iv. 7 It seemed as though they were sent forth as men doomed to death, and made a spectacle to the world, and to angels, and to men. But notwithstanding all, there was a peace which was absolutely independent of external conditions, whether of joy or sorrow. Is it not evident that the quality of their peace was infinitely higher than that which we have discussed? It had heights and depths, breadths and lengths, that passed the understanding of ordinary men.

Imagine an apostle coming to such a home as we have described—coming out of the storm of some terrible persecution, coming as a fugitive from a distant city, coming as Paul came to Athens from Berœa, and yet with the peace of God upon the face, the light of heaven shining in the eye, betraying the restful and calm demeanour of the tranquil soul. Would not the 'son of peace' who had carefully hedged himself around with every earthly barrier against discomfort and tribulation, realise that there was a Divine quality in the peace which kept the heart and mind of his visitor?

To return to the illustration already employed. Such peace may be well compared to the coming of ambassadors from the interior of the country on which the poor shipwrecked mariner has landed, to tell him that beyond the line of trees that guard the coast there is a friendly Emperor, that the country is Christian, that the people are hospitable, that there is awaiting him the goodwill of those with whom his lot would henceforth be cast. These Apostles of Christ, who breathed His peace, did not fear the unknown, since it was well known to Him ; did not fear the future, for it was present to Him ; were not startled at the change in circumstances, since their peace did not depend upon external things, but upon Him who is First and Last, and who guaranteed the supply of all need. Phil. iv. 7

This Peace is based upon the Work of Christ

'Christ is our Peace.' 'He has made peace by the Blood of His Cross.' He has come to us with the tidings that God is reconciled, and desires that we should be reconciled with Him ; He breaks down our stubborn rebellion, and brings us into harmony with the Father's will ; changes the heart of stone into the heart of flesh ; teaches us that our salvation does not depend on what we are to feel, but on the over-abounding love of God ; convinces us that He who has done so much for our salvation will not forget the body, with all its varied need, and opens up to us the heart of the Father, so true and tender, so set upon our help, that within its limits all fulness dwells, pledged to our supply.

It is the Peace that dwelt in the Heart of Jesus

All through the agitating scenes of our Lord's arrest and death, He bore Himself as one in whose heart the peace of God reigned in unbroken calm. He said : 'These things have I spoken unto you, that in Me ye may have peace. In the world ye shall have tribulation, but be of good cheer, I have overcome the world.' Spat upon, mocked, scourged, crucified, He never for a single moment lost His kingliness of mien. In the midst of the excitement in the garden, when being led forth as a felon, He was able to work a miracle on the ear of Malchus ; and when standing before Pilate, the royalty of His

Phil. iv. 7

manhood was so apparent, that the governor was convinced that He had done nothing amiss, and became His advocate. *My peace* He said, and says. The peace that filled His heart is His gift to all that are united with Him by a living faith.

This Peace is intended to keep our Hearts and Thoughts

The word *keep* is the term for sentry duty. It is as though the peace of God, like some sentinel angel, went to and fro before the portal of our inner life, keeping back all intruders who would break in upon the purity of our affections, or the integrity of our thoughts. How often we have been flurried and agitated! How suddenly things have broken in upon us which have rocked the waters of the inner lake to storm! How frequently the fever of the world has entered, for want of a disinfecting barrier, to raise the pulses of our souls to fever heat! But all this may be prevented when the peace that passeth understanding keeps us.

Conditions of Reception

The conditions of receiving this peace are threefold. *Be anxious for nothing.* 'Anxiety' comes from the same root as anger, and refers to the physical act of choking. Worry chokes the life of faith; it does not help us to meet our difficulties; so far from this it unfits us, for our mind is too flurried to think clearly and carefully, our hand trembles too much to perform the delicate operation. Therefore, the perpetual injunction of the New Testament to the children of God, is, as Jesus puts it, 'Take no anxious thought.' We must watch against it as against any other temptation; we must resist the first intimation of the overshadowing blight of care; we must turn from to-morrow's threatened difficulty to the face of God who is 'the same yesterday, to-day, and forever.' He will be there, and He will be for judgment when we have to sit in judgment and give our decisions as certainly as He will be for strength when we have to turn the battle from the gate. Phil. iv. 7

We are to be anxious about nothing, however great or trivial. The storm that threatens to engulf the house of our life, and the gnawing of the tiny mouse in the cellar; the bankruptcy which may sweep away the accumulation of years, and the few coins that we may have mislaid! Nothing in the whole range of our life should give us anxiety because there is nothing which is not within the circumference of God's care, nothing which gives us annoyance is too small for the notice of our Heavenly Father, who has a cure for every ailment, a foil for every weapon of the adversary.

Be prayerful about Every-thing

In everything by prayer and supplication let your requests be made known unto God. Prayer is more general, supplication more specific. Whenever the least shadow of care threatens our life we should go at once to our knees, and in the silence of private prayer hand over the burden and responsibility to our Infinite and All-wise Father. We have to make our requests known. Not that He will always give us what we ask, but will read into our prayers the meaning that we would put in them, were we as well informed as He is of what is best. There need not be undue urgency or excitement, or the play of profound emotion; in quietness and confidence will be our strength, the

Phil. iv. 7

least whisper will enter into the depths of God's nature, the tiniest tremor of our heart will be noticed, the least as well as the greatest of our demands will be met.

Be thankful for Anything

Go over the mercies of the past. Count your blessings; remember all the way which the Lord your God has led you; see how His loving-kindness has been encompassing your path and your lying down, your going out to service and your coming in to rest through long years. Has there not been a plan in your life? Are you not conscious of a Divine purpose? Do you not realise that the hand of the Potter has been moulding you into a vessel for His use? Is not the sweet reasonableness of many mysteries that once puzzled you beginning to reveal itself? Have you not a clue to the maze? As you stand on the eminence of the years, can you not see that the path by which you have come through the valley is the directest and safest? How much we have to be thankful for, how often we have been stayed on the very brink of ruin, how marvellously we have been withdrawn from the doing or saying that which would have shattered our usefulness! Oh my heart, take the harp from the willows, and commence where thou wilt to praise thy God; and as the song of praise begins to steal up in faltering notes at first, but with ever more certainty and thankfulness, the clouds will break, the chink of blue sky will widen until the whole vault of heaven is clear, and the peace of God like a pure, strong, beautiful angel will descend to act as sentry to the heart and mind,—to the *heart*, keeping out unholy affection, and to the *mind*, checking the entrance of rebellious, restless, and distracting thoughts. **Phil. iv. 7**

The Benediction of Peace

Those that have this peace can unlock its stores for others. It is as though, like Rebekah of old, they draw from deep wells, and are able to wet the lips of thirsty travellers from the overflowing of their buckets. Their presence calms, soothes, and quiets the restless and perturbed spirit. No such nurses for the sick room, no such confidants in hours of anxiety, no such strong and wise advisers in perplexity! The hand of the priest or minister can be stretched out to invoke upon the congregation the peace of God, but the people may go away uncomforted; whilst one quiet heart, which has drunk deep into the peace of Christ, radiates it forth with the velocity and virtue of the newly discovered metal radium.

Of course, such peace needs a quiet and sympathetic heart, able to appreciate and respond. As in wireless telegraphy, the instrument at the receiving must be in perfect harmony with that at the transmitting station; so there must be some knowledge of peace, some yearning desire for it, some reciprocity, if the Divine peace is to find entrance. The 'son of peace' receives the higher, purer quality which the apostle of peace brings. God ever says to these souls, 'Ye shall see greater things than these.' If He has given the nether, He will add the upper springs also.

But there are cases in which this reciprocity is withheld. 'Your peace shall return to you again.' The

Phil. iv. 7 salutation to peace excites the frown, the refusal, the chilling reply—what then! Is it lost? Nay, verily, it comes back to the heart from which it originated. The peace comes back to roost, as the dove to Noah's ark when the patriarch put forth his hand and took her in to himself; or as the waves dashing against the sea wall, and unable to effect an entrance through its stony barrier, return their unspent force to the heart of mother-ocean from which they sprang. Thus does the peace which we would communicate to others, but they will not receive, come back to our own hearts. Nothing is lost in this world which is done for God, and no word spoken for Him can be in vain. With infinite care He causes us to be enriched by the beneficence we intend for others, but which they will not receive.

24

THE GOVERNMENT OF OUR THOUGHTS

Philippians 4:8,9

FINALLY, brethren, whatsoever things are true, whatsoever things *are* honest, whatsoever things *are* just, whatsoever things *are* pure, whatsoever things *are* lovely, whatsoever things *are* of good report; if *there be* any virtue, and if *there be* any praise, think on these things.

Those things, which ye have both learned, and received, and heard, and seen in me, do: and the God of peace shall be with you.

Phil. iv. 8, 9

The God of Peace

WE last spoke about *the peace of God* which, like a white-robed sentry, keeps the heart with its affections, and thoughts, with all their busy and sometimes too promiscuous crowd. We have now to speak about *the God of peace;* and blessed though the peace of God may be, to have the God from whose nature peace emanates is infinitely preferable. One main constituent of our text is the word *think;* another the word *do.*

Thinking and doing are the conditions on which the God of peace will tarry in the heart. To think rightly, and to do rightly—these will bring the blessed dove of heaven to brood in the nest of your soul. Almost everything in life depends on the thoughts, as the forest lies in the acorn, and Scripture itself lays stress upon this. The wise man says: 'Keep thy heart with all diligence; for out of it are the issues of life;' and, again, we have it: 'As a man thinketh in his heart so is he.' In this context

Phil. iv. 8, 9

we notice that the peace of God is to keep our thoughts; and, again, our text says: 'Think on these things.' The control of your thought, the government of your mind, this is all important for three reasons.

Thinking and Doing

(1) *Because thinking about things prepares you for doing them.* If you allow a matter to revolve in your mind, if you turn it over and over and consider it from every aspect, and dwell upon it, it becomes comparatively easy to do it. It is as though the thoughts lay down the tram lines, upon which presently the car of action proceeds. The thoughts lay the wires which presently convey the message. No doubt many of you have again and again experienced this, that when you have come to some great crisis in your life, you have passed through it with perfect ease, because you had so often rehearsed the matter. When you came to act, it was as though you had passed through the experience before, your thought had so entirely prepared you for it. It is of the utmost importance therefore that you take care what you think, because thought is the precursor, herald, and forerunner of action.

Thought and Character

(2) *Thought is also important, because it has a reflex effect upon the whole character.* As you think, so you *are* almost without knowing it. Wordsworth refers to this; he says:—

> 'We live by admiration, love, and hope;
> As these are well and wisely fixed,
> In dignity of being we ascend.'

If a man cherishes bad thoughts, almost unwittingly he deteriorates; he cannot help it. There is a profound philosophy in Rom. i., where it says that because they refused to retain God in their minds, but cherished their vile lusts, God gave them up to their passions to defile themselves. If a man is perpetually cherishing unholy, impure, and untrue thoughts, he will become an unholy, impure, and untrue man. Our character takes on the complexion and hue of our inward thinking. If a man is ever cherishing noble thoughts, he cannot help becoming noble; if he is generous in his thought, he will be in his act; if he is loving and tender in his thought, he will be loving and tender in his bearing. Thoughts are the looms in the wonderful machinery of the inner life, which are running day and night, and weaving the garments in which the soul shall be arrayed. If you will care for your thoughts, the thought will mould character reflexively and unconsciously.

Phil. iv. 8, 9

Thought and Ideals

(3) *Thought affects us because we naturally pursue our ideals.* Columbus, after long thinking, came to the conclusion that the earth was round, and that conviction determined him to launch his little boat and steer westward. Washington thought that government must be based on universal suffrage and free vote of the people, and this led to the formation of the United States. Wilberforce thought that every man was equally free in the sight of God, created and redeemed to be responsible to God only, apart from the holding of his fellow-man. Young men and women may read these words in whom great thoughts are formulating themselves, and if

Phil. iv. 8, 9

they are not to be mere enthusiasts, mere weak dreamers, the time must come when they will yoke the car of their thought to the star of their ideal, and presently a life will tower up before their fellows that shall leave a definite impression for blessing upon the race. If you are to be any more than a dreamer and enthusiast, young friend, your thought must, sooner or later, take shape in your industry and energy, even in the sweat of your brow, and the suffering of martyrdom.

Thought often unnoticed

It is a remarkable touch in John Bunyan's description of Ignorance, as he walks beside the two elder pilgrims, that he says: 'My heart is as good as any man's heart'—and adds, 'As to my thoughts, I take no notice of them.' Probably there are scores of people who take no notice of their thoughts. They leave the castle gate of their soul perfectly open for any intruder that may wish to enter, either from heaven or hell; and so it befalls that the thoughts of the world, of vanity, of impurity, thoughts which are inspired by demons, but which are arrayed in the garb of respectable citizens, pour into the great gateway of the soul, filling the courtyard with their tumultuous uproar. Without discrimination, thought, or care on their part, they allow themselves to be occupied and possessed with thoughts of which they have every reason to be ashamed; they teem in and out, and do just as they will. This is the reason why you sometimes find your heart filled with passion; it is because Guy Fawkes has entered in disguise with his fellow-conspirators, and under long flowing robes has introduced explosives. This is why our hearts become filled with hatred, malice, and all uncharitableness, with thoughts against God, and against our fellows. We do not watch the great courtyard gate.

Phil. iv. 8, 9

Think reverently

Think carefully, think reverently, says the Apostle; take care how you think. We might almost say you can live as you like, if you are only careful how you think. At the great dock gates they will feel down the casual labourers before permitting them to enter the great warehouse, and again when they come out. We are told that in some of the great hospitals they will search the visitors, especially on Sunday afternoon, lest they should introduce deleterious food, which might neutralise the physicians' treatment. When there was the dynamite scare in London, how carefully the policemen examined everybody who had business in the House of Commons, lest a bomb might be introduced. If only we had a scrutator standing at the door of our heart to examine every thought as it entered; nay, if we could have there the Angel Ithuriel, of whom Milton speaks, and the touch of whose spear showed that the devil lurked in the toad that squatted by Eve's ear and whispered her his secret, how often in what seems a respectable thought entering the courtyard gate we should discover a traitor, who had come from the very pit to set our heart on fire with sin.

The Conflict of Thoughts

It would appear that to arrest the tide of evil thoughts that threatens us is what St. Paul means when he says he is crucified with Christ. When newly converted there is nothing that we suffer from so much as the collision between the intrusion of those

Phil. iv. 8, 9

thoughts and the new divine principle, which has entered us. Just for a few hours watch carefully at the gateway of your hearts, and see if it be not sometimes almost an agony to exclude those which you must suspect. In beginning to do this, many would learn, perhaps for the first time, what the Cross of Christ means. It might bring the very perspiration to your forehead, in the awful conflict against certain fascinating thoughts, so winsome, so bright, so attractive, that offer themselves with the most insinuating grace. In earlier days, when one's standard was not quite so high, when one was less aware of the insidious temptation that lurks in the most graceful and attractive thoughts, one would have permitted them to enter, but now how great a fight goes on at the great gate of the soul, not only against bold bad thoughts, but against the more pleasing and seductive ones.

* * *

But supposing we were left merely with this constant watching and antagonising of evil thoughts, life would be almost intolerable. *Remember, therefore, that not the negative only but the positive, not destruction only but construction, is the law of the Christian life.* Not the grave of Christ, but the resurrection power, is our hope; and hence St. Paul says, 'Think on these things'—and he gives you six standards of thoughts.

Think on the True

'Whatsoever things are *true*.' Keep out of your mind the false, but admit the true, because every life, every government, all politics, all business, all great commercial undertakings, all books and systems, which are not founded upon truth crumble sooner or later. If you could visit this world in the future, you would find that the falsehoods which now stalk across its arena, and seem as strong as thistles in spring, will have passed away. Consider things that are true. **Phil. iv. 8, 9**

On the Honourable

'Whatsoever things are *honourable.*' The word in the Greek is *grave*—reverent—respect-compelling—everything which is respectable, which makes for itself a court of respect. Exclude from your mind all that is dishonourable, and admit only what is worthy of God.

'Whatsoever things are *just.*' Be absolutely just to other people in your estimate, in giving them their dues. If they be above you, criticise them justly; if on your level, deal with them as you would wish them to deal with you; if beneath you, be just. Everything unjust in speech or habit prohibit; everything which is just foster.

On the Pure

'Whatsoever things are *pure.*' Here is the fight for a young man's life, to arrest the impure, however bedizened and bedecked, and to admit into his heart only that which is perfectly pure, pure as the lily, as God's ether, as the light.

On the Lovely

'Whatsoever things are *lovely.*' That conduct which is consistent with 1 Cor. xiii., which proceeds from the heart of love and thaws the ice of selfishness, which has accumulated upon others.

And on the Things of Good Report

'Whatsoever things are *of good report.*' Like the elders who obtained a good report; like Mary, of whom Jesus said, 'She hath done what she could;' like the man with his ten talents, to whom the Lord

Phil. iv. 8, 9

said, 'Well done, good and faithful servant.' Anything, the Apostle says, which is virtuous, and anything which wins praise of God or man, think on these things.

Let these six sisters stand at the gateway of your soul, and challenge every thought as it offers itself, admitting only those thoughts which approve themselves as true, just, pure, lovely, and of good report. O God, let these six angels come into our souls, and from now until we meet Thee, let us give the entire control of our nature up to their serene, strong, wholesome restraint, that all that is inconsistent with them may be abashed, and everything which is consistent with them admitted to infill and dwell within us.

A High Ideal

You say the ideal is high. Yes, but listen; we must believe that each of these attributes was won by Christ for us all—*won by Him.* They were native to Him, but they were won because He pursued them through temptation. He kept them as His own, face to face with the most terrific temptations ever presented to a moral being. Having endured all, He died, rose, and bore to God's right hand a humanity in which these things were eternal and inherent. Thence he sent down the Holy Spirit to reproduce His risen humanity in every one who believes.

But attainable by Faith

Faith is the power with which we receive through the Holy Ghost the nature of Jesus Christ into our hearts; so that instead of talking about justice, purity, and self-restraint as so many abstract qualities, we speak about Him in whom those attributes are incarnated. By faith we receive Him, and having received Him, we receive them. Let the Holy Spirit reproduce Him. Phil. iv. 8, 9

Just now we said, Let those six sisters stand at the gateway and test all our thoughts. But it is better to say, Let Jesus Christ stand at the gateway and test them, because He can not only test but roll back the tide of evil thought, as easily as He could make Niagara leap back, did He choose. It is mere stoicism and stoical philosophy to say: Watch your thoughts. It is Christian philosophy to say: Let Christ keep your thoughts, testing them, hurling back the evil, and filling the soul with His glorious presence.

This is the secret of the indwelling presence of the God of Peace. He abides where the heart is kept free from evil thoughts, and filled with the Spirit of the Son. 'The God of Peace shall be with you.'

25

ALL THINGS ARE POSSIBLE TO HIM THAT BELIEVETH

Philippians 4:10-13

BUT I rejoiced in the Lord greatly, that now at the last your care of me hath flourished again; wherein ye were also careful, but ye lacked opportunity.

Not that I speak in respect of want: for I have learned, in whatsoever state I am, *therewith* to be content.

I know both how to be abased, and I know how to abound: every where and in all things I am instructed both to be full and to be hungry, both to abound and to suffer need.

I can do all things through Christ which strengtheneth me.

Phil. iv. 10-13

FOR ten years the Philippian Church had been unable to send material aid to its beloved founder. It was not because his love for them, or theirs to him had cooled, but they had lacked opportunity. Previously, his friends had contributed, even beyond their power, to aid him in relieving the need of their poorer brethren in Judea. In addition to this, they had sent, 'once and again,' to relieve his personal wants. Then for some time their help had ceased; but just recently, in his sore destitution during his Roman imprisonment, their love for him had flamed out in generous bounty, and they had sent by Epaphroditus, substantial proof that their care for him had flourished again.

Bound: Received with Joy

This was a matter of great satisfaction to the much-tried Apostle. It touched his generous nature; it was an evidence that the love he so greatly prized, was as fresh and strong as ever. It seemed to him that the Master Himself was gratified with the sacrifices they had made; but he hastened to add, that they must not for a moment suppose that he was dependent upon outward gifts for contentment and peace. His secret of happiness was not in circumstances, but in his peace of heart; he would not admit that his joy was lessened when his circumstances were more straitened, and enhanced when they brimmed with comfort. His serenity lay beyond the range of storms, in Christ. The secret of the Lord was with him, the high mountains of God's protection defended from ruffling alarm the lake of the inner life, he possessed the white stone, with the name written on it. He wanted them to understand that he did not for a moment reflect on their long silence, or speak in respect of want, for he had 'learned in whatsoever state he was, therewith to be content.' **Phil. iv. 10-13**

Contentment desirable in this World of Fluctuation

It has been said, that contentment produces in some measure all the effects which the alchemist usually ascribes to the philosopher's stone; and if it does not bring riches, it achieves the same object by banishing the desire for them. How true this is. We become rich either by possessing the abundance of this world, or by losing our desire for it, by abounding in everything, or by being content to have nothing; and surely of the two conditions, in such a changeful world as this, the latter is both safer and happier.

The world is constantly compared to the sea, with its fluctuation of tide, its alternation of storm and

Phil. iv. 10-13

calm. We are reminded by Isaiah of 'the troubled sea which cannot rest,' and unhappy are they whose all is embarked upon this troublous scene, having no fixity of tenure, no stability of possession, but driven by the wild winds of change, and often of panic. To have little and to be content with it, is better far than to have great riches invested in the Stock Exchange, where a man may be a millionaire to-day and a pauper to-morrow. Well may the Apostle, in another and later Epistle, speak of 'uncertain riches,' and urge the disciples not to trust in them, but in the Living God 'who gives richly all things to enjoy.' Often, in human experience, the mountains are carried into the heart of the seas, the waters roar and are troubled, and the rocks are shaken by the swelling waters; but how good it is at such times to frequent the banks of the river, whose streams make glad the city of God, and whose placid upper waters reflect the jasper of God's throne! To be independent of circumstances, to set them at defiance, to be as happy when hungry as when filled, to be at rest when suffering need as when abounding, to resemble the compass which is so swung as to be unaffected by the motion of the ship, to have the jewel of a Divine peace which the thieving hands of anxiety and care cannot touch, surely, only thus can we discover the gleam of a life which is no longer at the mercy of the elements, but resembles the shaft of light which penetrates the murky cloud, and strikes through the storm itself, but is too ethereal to be disturbed by the rush of the wind or the dash of the foaming breaker.

All Things are Possible

Where shall we find it? Where barns are full of grain, and the sheds of cattle? Where mansions overlook miles of parkland and landscape? Where the feet sink ankle-deep in the rich piles of the carpets, and upholsterers have done their utmost to furnish the rooms with dazzling elegance; where the murmur of the outer world hardly enters, and where distracting care has no twig on which to perch? Not there. When human life is surrounded by every circumstance of comfort and luxury, it is very often fullest of *ennui*, complaining and discontent!

Phil. iv. 10-13

Such Contentment is oftenest found where least expected

The causes for it may be ignoble and superficial—that some other beauty outshines, that some other house is more splendidly furnished, that some other life attracts more notoriety, that there is a touch of frost in the air to-day, or a degree or two more of heat.

If we would find content, let us go to homes where women are crippled with rheumatism, or dying of cancer, where comforts are few, where long hours of loneliness are not broken by the intrusion of friendly faces, where the pittance of public charity hardly suffices for necessary need, to say nothing of comfort, it is there that contentment reveals itself like a shy flower. How often in the homes of the wealthy one has missed it, to find it in the homes of the poor! How often it is wanting where health is buoyant, to be discovered where disease is wearing out the strength! So it was with the Apostle, who was in the saddest part of his career. Bound to the Roman soldier, enclosed in some narrow apartment, in touch with only a few friends who made an effort

Phil. iv. 10-13

to discover him, away from the happy scenes of earlier years, and anticipating Nero's bar, he breaks out into these glorious expressions of equanimity. He had learned how to be abased in the valley of shadow, he wore the flower heartsease in his buttonhole.

Contentment pre-eminently a Christian Grace

The idea of it has been always present to the minds of men, but the power by which the ideal could be realised has been lacking. For instance, Cicero who wrote volumes of incitement to courage and manly virtue, when he was driven into exile, though it was by no means onerous, wearied his friends with puerile and unmanly murmurings. It was the same with Seneca, whose books are full of stoic endurance and superiority to suffering, but as soon as he was exiled from Rome, he filled the air with abject complaints, and was not ashamed to fall at the feet of a worthless freedman to induce him to procure a revocation of his exile and permission to return from Sardinia to the metropolis.

How different was the great Apostle! Though deprived of every comfort, and cast as a lonely man on the shores of the great strange metropolis, with every movement of his hand clanking a fetter, and nothing before him but the lion's mouth or the sword, he speaks serenely of contentment.

Paul's Contentment was not complacency with himself

In the previous chapter, he tells us that he had not attained, but was following after. He refused to be content with what he had already accomplished for himself or others, his whole soul was on fire to apprehend more absolutely that for which Christ had apprehended him, but whilst he could not be content with the spiritual attainment or service, he was absolutely content with the circumstances of his lot. Looking up into the face of Jesus, he confessed his discontent; looking around at the prison, the gaoler, and the future, since these were all contained in the will of God for him, he was absolutely satisfied, because infinite love had permitted them.

Phil. iv. 10-13

Nor indifference to the state of the world around him

He longed that men might be turned from darkness to light, and from the power of Satan to God. He could never be content until his Master was the enthroned King of the world; and strove with unabating determination, according to the working of the mighty Spirit of God, 'to present every man perfect in Christ Jesus.' His eager spirit participated in the very travail of Christ for His body's sake, the Church. He was willing to be accursed for his brethren, the unbelieving Jews. But amid all this, he was content with the poor raft on which he was navigating the stormy seas. It was enough for him that God had willed his circumstances, and that Christ was his partner and friend. His was the spirit of the Psalmist, when he said, 'Whom have I in heaven but Thee, and there is none on earth beside Thee? My heart and flesh faileth, but God is the strength of my heart, and my portion for ever.'

Paul had learned the Art

Just as our Lord 'learned obedience by the things that He suffered,' so the Apostle acquired the habit of contentment by practising it. He had schooled himself, by constantly applying the Cross of Jesus to his ambitions, his murmurings, his tendency to complain. He had accustomed himself to dwell

Phil. iv. 10-13

upon the bright side of things, to lay more stress upon what he had than upon what he lacked. It was the habit of his life to take his lot from God, to look upon it as illumined by perfect wisdom and perfect love. He refused to listen to the dark and sinister suggestions flung into his soul by the tempter. Yes, we can do a great deal to elaborate the faculty of contentment; the germ of it is in our hearts by the grace of God, but the flower and fruit demand our constant heed.

Three Conditions for the Grace of Contentment: (1) We must live in the Will of God

All is of God, and God is good. Every wind blows from the quarter of His love, every storm wafts us nearer the harbour, every cup, though presented by the hand of Judas, is mixed by the Father of our spirits. It is not possible for a man to be thrust by his brethren in the pit, unless God permit it, and therefore we may say with Joseph, 'It was not you that sent me hither, but God.' Habituate yourself, oh Christian soul, to believe that not only what God appoints but what He permits, is in the sphere of His will! It is His will for you to be full to-day or to be empty to-morrow; to abound to-day or to be abased to-morrow; He has a reason, though He may not tell it, and because you know that the reason satisfies *Him*, *you* may be content.

(2) We must turn to Christ as the complement of our Need

Jesus Christ is sufficient. The greater our lack, the larger our supply. 'To them that have no might He increaseth strength.' To the ignorant He is wisdom, to the unholy sanctification, to the enslaved redemption. His miracles manifested the supply of His royal nature to the need around Him;

His purity cleansed the polluted flesh of the leper; His life poured into the arteries of death; His strength made good the helplessness of the paralysed. Receive from Christ 'grace upon grace,' and look upon the emptiness and need of your spirit as the greater reason why you should claim all from Him.

Phil. iv. 10-13

(3) We must do all things in Christ's Strength

The prophet Isaiah says, that 'they that wait upon the Lord *change* their strength' (Isa. xl. 31, A.V. margin). They begin life with the strength of young manhood, which boasts that it is well able to realise its dreams with its natural vigour, but as life goes on they tire and faint, the youths faint and are weary, the young men utterly fall. Then it is that they learn to avail themselves of the strength of the Everlasting God, the Creator of the ends of the earth, 'Who fainteth not, neither is weary.' Moses no longer trusts in the blow of his mailed fist, but by faith feeds his soul from the fountains of omnipotence; Peter no longer vaunts his ability to follow Christ even to death, but receives the power and anointing of the Holy Ghost, and becomes bold as a lion; Paul no longer speaks of his Pharisaic ancestry, and all the qualities which he had counted so much gain, but is content to be weak with Christ, that with Christ he may receive and depend upon the power of God. This change must come to us all. Whatever our need, we must turn for its supply to the fulness of God in Christ. As we keep open the avenue of our soul to our Lord, He will pour His strength into our nerveless and helpless nature. Nay, He will not merely give us His strength, but will be in us the power of God unto salvation. We

Phil. iv. 10-13 need not simply the strength of Christ, but Christ who gives strength, that we may be able to say with the Apostle, 'I can do all things'—whether it is to live or die, whether it is to be abased or abound, whether it is to be full or empty—'through Christ that strengtheneth me.'

Practice these three conditions, and you will learn, perhaps in dark hours of trial, and on the hard benches of the school of affliction, the art of contentment which shall enrich your life more than if the mines of Ophir were unlocked for your wealth.

26

FILLING AND FILLED

Philippians 4:14-20

NOTWITHSTANDING ye have well done, that ye did communicate with my affliction.

Now ye Philippians know also, that in the beginning of the gospel, when I departed from Macedonia, no church communicated with me as concerning giving and receiving, but ye only.

For even in Thessalonica ye sent once and again unto my necessity.

Not because I desire a gift: but I desire fruit that may abound to your account.

But I have all, and abound: I am full, having received of Epaphroditus the things *which were sent* from you, an odour of a sweet smell, a sacrifice acceptable, wellpleasing to God.

But my God shall supply all your need according to His riches in glory by Christ Jesus.

Now unto God and our Father *be* glory for ever and ever. Amen.

THE Apostle had already made it clear, that though **Phil. iv. 14-20** for a long interval he had received nothing from the Philippian Church, he did not complain, but realised that there were sufficient reasons which accounted for the cessation of their gifts. He did not deny that he had been straitened in outward circumstances, but he had been content because he discerned the will of God in every dispensation, and was able to do all things in union with the Living Christ. He had found that his legitimate necessities had been met, and that God had dealt with him as with Elijah, to whom the feathered fowl, and the

Phil. iv. 14-20

slender resources of the widow of Zarephath, ministered daily provision. He rejoiced, however, that his friends had been able to send again to his necessity, not for his sake alone, but for theirs, It was not that he sought for a gift, but for fruit that might be reckoned to their account.

The Gift and its Return

No Church had done for Paul what the Philippian Church had. In the early days they had sent once and again to minister to his need; and now their present, forwarded by the hand of Epaphroditus, redounded still further to their credit. It was 'an odour of a sweet smell, a sacrifice acceptable, well-pleasing to God.' How could he repay them for the gifts they had sent when they were able, and for the desire to send when they were not. It was clear that he must always be hopelessly in debt to them so far as material supplies were concerned, but he could pray and make intercession on their behalf, and remind the Master that all kindness shown to the servant imposed an honourable obligation on the Master, and out of all this arose the assurance that his 'God would fulfil every need of theirs according to His riches in glory in Christ Jesus.'

'Fulfil'

To translate the Greek word as R.V. does by *fulfil* connects this verse with the preceding one, and brings out the designed and beautiful harmony. The Apostle was filled because he had received from Epaphroditus the gifts of his friends, and now God would fulfil their need. What they had done in the lower sphere for him would be repeated in a higher sphere by God. The measure with which they had meted out their stores for the imprisoned Apostle would be returned to them brimming to the full, not with the supplies for physical need, but with the eternal and unsearchable riches of heaven, which are in Christ Jesus. Phil. iv. 14-20

Give and Receive

This is a constant law of God's world. 'Give, and it shall be given unto you: good measure, pressed down, shaken together, running over, shall be given into your bosom. For with what measure ye mete, it shall be measured to you again.' Lend your boat for a whole afternoon to Christ that it may be His floating pulpit, and He will return it to you laden with fish. Place your upper room at His disposal for a single meal, and He will fill it and the whole house with the Holy Spirit of Pentecost. Place in His hands your barley loaves and fish, and He will not only satisfy your hunger, but add twelve baskets full of fragments. The Philippians sent three or four presents to a suffering and much needing servant of God, and from that moment they might reckon that every need of theirs would be supplied. Such small acts on our part are recompensed with such vast returns. We scratch the surface of the soil and insert our few little seeds, and within a few months the acreage is covered by a prolific harvest in which a hundredfold is given for every grain which we seemed to throw away.

God's Return to Us

God refuses to be in debt to any man. He takes into His exchequer the accounts of all outlay made by His stewards for the relief of need and distress, and He repays with interest. When the Good Samaritan was leaving the village inn, on the morning after the memorable rescue of the wounded

Phil. iv. 14-20

traveller, he said to the host, 'Take care of him, and what thou spendest more, when I come again, I will repay.' Evidently, he was well-known on the road, he had often been at that inn before, and had established his character by honourable and generous treatment. They knew that his word was his bond, and that whatever was expended in reason would secure an ungrudging repayment. And if this be true of man how much more of God. He hands over to us cases in which He is deeply interested, saying as He does so, 'Take care of these, expend what is necessary, and I will repay.' May we not reckon on God for this? According to our faith it will be to us.

But give cheerfully

Whenever, therefore, we feel impelled to make provision for others, let us do it as unto God, not simply out of human pity, but from a deep sense of obligation to our Heavenly Father, let us do it gladly, freely, generously. 'God loveth a cheerful giver.' Three things will happen—(1) We shall send a thrill of gratitude into some weary and fainting soul, encouraging it to hope in God because it has found that its hope in man has not been misplaced. (2) The odour of the act will be fragrant as it steals upward to mingle with the adoration and service of Heaven. There is no longer need to offer propitiatory sacrifices, for they have been done away in view of the sacrifice made by our Lord when He once offered Himself without sin unto God, but there is room in the Christian dispensation for the sacrifice of praise (Heb. xiii. 15), for the living sacrifice of ourselves (Rom. xii. 1), and for the acceptable sacrifices of Christian beneficence which, as this paragraph tells us, are well-pleasing to God. (3) We may also reckon that He will fill to the brim the measure with which we have meted out for others, and take it as a certainty that He shall fulfil every need according to His riches. If our measure was filled with sand grains, He will return it filled with gold dust; if it was filled with pebbles, He will hand it back replete with diamonds; if it contained necessaries for the physical life, He will restore it brimming over with spiritual riches. **Phil. iv. 14-20**

Charity succeeded by Poverty

It may be answered that many who have given lavishly for God's cause have afterwards come to penury and need, and their benefactions seem to have been lost like argosies that go down at sea. In any case, there has been no return to brighten the straitened circumstances of declining years. Three answers may be given. First, it may be that the gifts were not rendered with a single eye for the glory of God, but for some lower motives of display, ostentation, or self-advertisement; therefore, they had their reward. They were done to be seen of men, they received the recognition and applause of men, and God refused to recognise any obligation for further recompense.

Secondly, it is necessary, before these laws of the spiritual world operate on our behalf, that we should definitely and by faith appropriate them. There is no promise which does not require to be claimed. As the angel of electricity will not step forth to illumine our rooms unless we turn the switch when we pass through the door, so we must not complain

Phil. iv. 14-20

that the laws of the spiritual world do not bring us help unless by faith we appropriate their service. Whenever, therefore, we expend alms for the relief of need, let us definitely put our money into God's bags, which wax not old: we should specifically lay up treasure in heaven, we should pay our money, so to speak, into the bank of His faithfulness, and reckon that there will be a definite return. It may be taken as an axiom that in this world there is a return for every gift that we lay on the altar of self-sacrifice—not of reward but of free grace. We must not make the gift in order to get the reward, but having made the gift in the name of Christ, and for the fulfilment of His redemptive purpose, we may certainly believe that in ways that we may not be able to define God will supply all our need.

Thirdly, it should be borne in mind that though there may be apparent straitness, there may be a wealth of content, a gold mine of peace and joy, the precious stones of spiritual grace, which correspond to the riches in glory of which the Apostle speaks. When life was young, they gave of their temporal things, and now as the evening shades gather, God gives them not temporalities but spiritualities. They sowed carnal things and reap spiritual ones (1 Cor. ix. 11).

God's Return

'All your need.' From the moment that we draw our first breath in this world to the last sigh of expiring life, we are full of needs. The babe has its cradle needs, and the patriarch those that arise from the wearing out of his faculties, and his growing dependence on others. The body has physical need, the mind its hunger for truth, the heart its insatiable longing for love, the spirit for spiritual sustenance and quickening. Our human nature is one great bundle of need, it is always crying aloud for satisfaction; and as civilisation advances, the variety and multiplicity of our need is ever on the increase. **Phil. iv. 14-20**

Needs and Desires

We must distinguish between our needs and our desires. It is possible to want a good many things which we do not need. We often want things which it would injure us greatly to have. Paul wanted to be delivered from his thorn, but his real need was for more grace. We want a great many things which it is not possible for our Heavenly Father to give us, except to the great detriment of our best life. There is no promise that God shall supply all our desires or wishes, there is a certainty that He will fulfil all our *need.*

Some may read these words whose needs are clamant,—the need for guidance, for help against temptation, for the quickening of languishing devotional life, the need for daily bread or employment. Let all such take this to their heart for their comfort that God will supply all their need. 'My God shall fulfil *every* need of yours.'

Christ is God's Answer to our Need

'In Him are all the treasures of wisdom and knowledge hidden.' 'It pleased the Father that in Him should all the fulness dwell.' 'In Him dwelleth all the fulness of the Godhead bodily.' The Divine-Human nature of Christ is replete with every possible supply for His people. 'He filleth all in all.' Those that trust Him can say, as the Apostle did of the Philippian gifts, 'I have all things and abound; I am filled, having received from Christ the things that

Phil. iv. 14-20

came from God, and which were treasured in Him for my enrichment and thanksgiving.' The teaching of the Apostle is full of this thought, as when he says, 'I thank my God always concerning you, for the grace of God which was given you in Christ Jesus; that in everything ye were enriched in Him" (1 Cor. i. 4, 5), and again, 'Blessed be the God and Father of our Lord Jesus Christ who hath blessed us with every spiritual blessing in the heavenly places in Christ' (Eph. i. 3). Peter also affirms the same thought. 'Grace to you, and peace be multiplied in the knowledge of God, and of Jesus our Lord; seeing that His Divine power hath granted unto us all things that pertain unto life and godliness' (2 Peter i. 2, 3).

Christ is the complement (*i.e.*, the completement of every soul). Just as the dark face of the moon taken with her first crescent of light makes a complete circle, so the unseen Redeemer together with our infinite need makes a complete man after God's stature. The greater our deficiency the larger His supply.

The Prime Necessity

The prime necessity, however, is that we should reckon it is so, and avail ourselves of all the treasures that are prepared for our use in our Risen Lord. Too often we act as if we had to meet the demands of life from our own limited exchequer, instead of believing that we have been taken into partnership with the Son of God, and can at any moment draw upon His all-sufficiency. What would you think if a clerk, who was sent to a distant land to open a branch of some great business firm, were to seek to meet the expenses out of his own limited salary, when the head of the firm had told him to draw upon his credit to any extent which he deemed necessary? But we make the same mistake when we meet the calls of life apart from the boundless wealth which is placed to our credit in Jesus.

Phil. iv. 14-20

A story is told by Dr Richard Newton of an old and poverty-stricken Indian, who many years ago made his way into a Western settlement in search of food to keep him from starving. A bright coloured ribbon was seen around his neck, from which there hung a small, dirty pouch. On being asked what it was, he said it was a charm given him in his younger days. He opened it, and took out a worn and crumpled paper, which he handed to the person making the inspection. It proved, on examination, to be a regular discharge from the federal army, signed by George Washington himself, and entitling him to a pension for life. Here was a man with a promise duly signed, which if presented in the right place would have secured him ample provision, yet he was wandering about hungry, helpless, and forlorn, and begging bread to keep him from starving. What a picture of many Christians who are in need of everything when they might be rich and full! Perhaps their own life has not been generous, certainly their faith has never put in its claim to God's great bank of promise.

We deal with a Father

Let us remember that we are dealing with a *Father*. 'Now unto our God and Father be the glory for ever.' The Father's eye is on His children, and a Father's hand is stretched out to their relief. Let us be of good cheer. Two sparrows are sold for

Phil. iv. 14-20

a farthing, but five for two farthings, that is, sparrows are so cheap that one can be thrown into the bargain, but that odd sparrow cannot fall to the ground without the notice of the Father. Surely we are of more value than many sparrows, and we may count on Him with absolute certainty. Nowhere in the world does He make birds, fish, young lions, or babes, without supplying the food which He has taught them to require. He cannot do worse by us; we dare not think that He has implanted needs which He is unable and unwilling to meet. Only let us make Him our confidant, going through life with a free-handed generosity that gives, and with an absolute trust which takes, making our requests known unto Him, and receiving the fulfilment of every need, out of which shall arise to Him who loves us, cares for us, and sustains us, glory unto the ages of the ages.

27

CLOSING SALUTATIONS

Philippians 4:21-23

SALUTE every saint in Christ Jesus. The brethren which are with me greet you.

All the saints salute you, chiefly they that are of Cæsar's household.

The grace of our Lord Jesus Christ *be* with you all. Amen.

¶ It was written to the Philippians from Rome by Epaphroditus.

Phil. iv. 21-23

PROBABLY, at this point, the Apostle took in hand the style with which his amanuensis had been rapidly penning his glowing thoughts, that in the clumsy letters, to which he refers in the Epistle of Galatians (vi. 11), probably due to his defective eyesight, he might append his autograph.

The Universality of his Greetings

'Salute every saint in Christ Jesus.' There were many distinctions between the disciples in that distant city. Some who professed a lofty spirituality, but lacked the spirit of loving concord; some who were tinctured with the pharisaic disputations of his own earlier days; and some who were able to appreciate the deepest teachings of the nature of Christ which human words can unfold. It was enough, however, that they were in Christ Jesus, that He had accepted them, and that already they were separated from the corruption that is in the world through lust, and were set apart for the glorious purpose of the Son of God, and therefore,

Phil. iv. 21-23

their faithful friend was able to include them all in his tender salutation.

How good it is when Christian love enables us to rise above sectarian strife, and the misunderstandings which are generated by the differences of our temperament and education, so that we are able to view each other as common members of the Body, and contiguous branches of the Vine, praying for each other, and prepared to communicate grace by word and act. Let us salute *every* saint, whether belonging to our own Church, or to some other. It is enough to know that they with us are partakers of the grace of God, and if He loves, there must be something lovable upon which our hearts can fasten.

* * *

Paul's Humility

There is no trace of the priest in these simple words. Having sent his own personal greetings, he hastens to class with himself his colleagues, as Timothy and Mark, or his travelling companions, as Luke and Silas, or prominent believers who dwelt in Rome, and had the right of entrance into his hired room. They were brethren more or less unknown, but the Apostle recognised that they had as much right to salute the saints in Philippi as he had, and he hastened to strengthen his own message by the inclusion of their good-will.

It is interesting to notice how fond the Apostle was of having others with him in his Christian work. Their fellowship gave him strength and comfort. Probably, he entered into the Spirit of the Master, who sent His disciples out two and two. Sometimes, he allied himself with Barnabas, at other times with Silas, at other times with Mark. The opening words of this Epistle show how closely he was associated with Timothy, 'his own son in the faith.' Two are better than one. It is a matter of great encouragement and strength when some kindred soul is united with us in any service.

Phil. iv. 21-23

* * *

The Gathering Wealth of Christian Love

'All the saints salute you.' The Apostle first salutes for himself; then he associates the brethren that were with him; and now his voice seems to have stirred a large circle of consenting hearts, and from them all a torrent of tender affection sets in towards the Philippian Church. There is every probability that the saints who here send greeting are those who themselves had been greeted and mentioned by name in Romans xvi. Bishop Lightfoot, in an essay on this passage which is full of interest, has pointed out that many of the names mentioned by Paul in the last chapter of his letter to the Romans are identical with the names deciphered in sepulchral inscriptions, and known to have had a place in the Imperial household. Of these he specifies Ampliatus, Apelles, Stachys, Rufus and Hermes, and the two women, Tryphæna and Tryphosa. These were almost certainly included in '*all* the saints.'

Thus this Epistle, so full of love, seems like a shuttle to have shot between these far removed centres of Christian life, uniting each to the other. Epaphroditus had brought a sweet savour of Philippi unto Rome, now this letter carries the fragrance of Roman Christianity to Philippi. It is thus that the

Churches in all ages have exchanged words and actions of Christian courtesy.

* * *

The Saints that are specially distinguished

'Especially them that are of Cæsar's household.' The great commentator already referred to, has shown that the household of Cæsar was a term embracing a vast number of persons, not only in Rome, but in the provinces, all of whom were either actual or former slaves of the Emperor, and filled every possible description of office. There is every reason to believe that this term included household slaves who were in immediate attendance upon the Emperor; soldiers who through being attached to the prisoner had been constrained to hear the story of salvation, and yielded to the claims of Jesus: and perhaps beyond, there was a still wider circle of senators and knights, men of intellectual power and large wealth, who composed the Imperial retinue and court. The household of Cæsar was constituted by a vast concourse, many of whom were the agents of murders, bitter cruelties, and licentious intrigues, but large numbers of whom were men of upright character, who found it possible, amid such surroundings as those of Nero's palace, to be simple followers of Jesus. It is as possible to be a Christian in a royal court as in a slum, in a fashionable circle as amongst peasants and labourers, amongst rulers as amongst the poor and destitute. Character may be independent of circumstances. Joseph may pursue his life of purity amid the corruption of Egypt, and Daniel his life of prayer amid the idolatry of Babylon.

Closing Salutations

Circumstances may differ; in some cases they are more, whilst in others they are less favourable to the growth of Christian character, but Christianity is indigenous to all climates, and will flourish on any soil. It is like the corn plant which grows alike upon the alluvial soil of the Nile Delta, and the broad expanse of Western prairies. **Phil. iv. 21-23**

It speaks much for the earnestness of individual workers in those early days, when there were no great conventions, nor many eloquent and commanding preachers, that such vast multitudes of believers were being gathered in every part of the known world through the individual effort of those who, like the first apostles, could say, 'Come and see.'

*   *   *

The Final Benediction

'The grace of the Lord Jesus Christ be with your spirit.' The Epistle begins with grace (v. 2) and with grace it ends. It is impossible to define all that is meant by this comprehensive prayer. Illumination for the soul, love for the heart, strength for the mind, purity for the character, help in every time of need, direction in all perplexity and difficulty—all these are included in the word grace. It was impossible for the Apostle to know in detail all that his friends might be passing through amid the temptations and perils of Philippi, but he wished that always and everywhere, they might be conscious that the grace of the Lord Jesus beset them behind and before, encompassed their going out and coming in, enwrapped them in their lying down and rising up, canopied them with skies opening Godward, and was their shield and their exceeding great reward.

F.B. MEYER MEMORIAL LIBRARY

Devotional Commentary on Exodus

This descriptive, directive and devotional work will be a special help to the hungry soul, the busy pastor, the pressured evangelist, the weighted missionary, and the searching scholar. 476 pages.

Choice Notes on Joshua—2 Kings

F.B. Meyer designed the book to record understandable, accessable notes on the books of Joshua through 2 Kings. The reader will gain new insight and challenge for today from these Old Testament books. 208 pages.

Choice Notes on the Psalms

This chapter-by-chapter commentary examines the Psalms from three perspectives: the historical setting, featuring the inner struggle of David; the prophetical references to Christ; and the practical applications. 192 pages.

Devotional Commentary on Philippians

The compressed and profound teaching of Philippians is X-rayed in this verse-by-verse commentary. This popular devotional is characterized by loyalty to the Scriptures and applications to the needs of today's believer. 262 pages.